Call me Ishmael

CHARLES OLSON

Call me Ishmael

CITY LIGHTS BOOKS

I wish to acknowledge the grant of a fellowship from the John Simon
Guggenheim Foundation to do this book.

Library of Congress Catalog Card Number: 58-5531

*CITY LIGHT BOOKS are published at the City Lights Bookstore,
261 Columbus Avenue, San Francisco, California 94111.*

O fahter, fahter
gone amoong

O eeys that loke

Loke, fahter:
your sone!

CONTENTS

FIRST FACT as prologue

FIRST FACT

Herman Melville was born in New York August 1, 1819, and on the 12th of that month the *Essex*, a well-found whaler of 238 tons, sailed from Nantucket with George Pollard, Jr. as captain, Owen Chase and Matthew Joy mates, 6 of her complement of 20 men Negroes, bound for the Pacific Ocean, victualled and provided for two years and a half.

A year and three months later, on November 20, 1820, just south of the equator in longitude 119 West, this ship, on a calm day, with the sun at ease, was struck head on twice by a bull whale, a spermeceti about 85 feet long, and with her bows stove in, filled and sank.

Her twenty men set out in three open whaleboats for the coast of South America 2000 miles away. They had bread

(200 lb. a boat), water (65 gallons), and some Galapagos turtles. Although they were at the time no great distance from Tahiti, they were ignorant of the temper of the natives and feared cannibalism.

Their first extreme sufferings commenced a week later when they made the mistake of eating, in order to make their supply last, some bread which had got soaked by the sea's wash. To alleviate the thirst which followed, they killed turtle for its blood. The sight revolted the stomachs of the men.

In the first weeks of December their lips began to crack and swell, and a glutinous saliva collected in the mouth, intolerable to the taste.

Their bodies commenced to waste away, and possessed so little strength they had to assist each other in performing some of the body's weakest functions. Barnacles collected on the boats' bottoms, and they tore them off for food. A few flying fish struck their sails, fell into the boats, and were swallowed raw.

After a month of the open sea they were gladdened by the sight of a small island which they took to be Ducie but was Elizabeth Isle. Currents and storm had taken them a thousand miles off their course.

They found water on the island after a futile search for it from rocks which they picked at, where moisture was, with their hatchets. It was discovered in a small spring in the sand at the extreme verge of ebbtide. They could gather it only at low water. The rest of the time the sea flowed over the spring to the depth of six feet.

Twenty men could not survive on the island and, to give themselves the chance to reach the mainland before the supplies they had from the ship should be gone, seventeen of them put back to sea December 27th.

The three who stayed, Thomas Chapple of Plymouth, England, and William Wright and Seth Weeks of Barnstable, Mass., took shelter in caves among the rocks. In one they found eight human skeletons, side by side as though they had lain down and died together.

The only food the three had was a sort of blackbird which they caught when at roost in trees and whose blood they sucked. With the meat of the bird, and a few eggs, they chewed a plant tasting like peppergrass which they found in the crevices of the rocks. They survived.

The three boats, with the seventeen men divided among them, moved under the sun across ocean together until the 12th of January when, during the night, the one under the command of Owen Chase, First Mate, became separated from the other two.

Already one of the seventeen had died, Matthew Joy, Second Mate. He had been buried January 10th. When Charles Shorter, Negro, out of the same boat as Joy, died on January 23rd, his body was shared among the men of that boat and the Captain's, and eaten. Two days more and Lawson Thomas, Negro, died and was eaten. Again two days and Isaac Shepherd, Negro, died and was eaten. The bodies were roasted to dryness by means of fires kindled on the ballast sand at the bottom of the boats.

Two days later, the 29th, during the night, the boat which had been Matthew Joy's got separated from the Captain's and was never heard of again. When she disappeared three men still lived, William Bond, Negro, Obed Hendricks, and Joseph West.

In the Captain's boat now alone on the sea, four men kept on. The fifth, Samuel Reed, Negro, had been eaten for strength at his death the day before. Within three days these four men, calculating the miles they had to go, decided to draw two lots, one to choose who should die that the others might live, and one to choose who should kill him. The youngest, Owen Coffin, serving on his first voyage as a cabin boy to learn his family's trade, lost. It became the duty of Charles Ramsdale, also of Nantucket, to shoot him. He did, and he, the Captain and Brazilla Ray, Nantucket, ate him.

That was February 1, 1821. On February 11th, Ray died of himself, and was eaten. On February 23rd, the Captain and Ramsdale were picked up by the Nantucket whaleship *Dauphin,* Captain Zimri Coffin.

The men in the third boat, under the command of Owen Chase, the first mate, held out the longest. They had become separated from the other two boats before hunger and thirst had driven any of the *Essex's* men to extremity. Owen Chase's crew had buried their first death, Richard Peterson, Negro, on January 20th.

It was not until February 8th, when Isaac Cole died in convulsions, that Owen Chase was forced, some two weeks later than in the other boats, to propose to his two men, Benjamin Lawrence and Thomas Nickerson, that they should eat of their own flesh. It happened to them this once, in this way: they separated the limbs from the body, and cut all the flesh from the bones, after which they opened the body, took out the heart, closed the body again, sewed it up as well as they could, and committed it to the sea.

They drank of the heart and ate it. They ate a few pieces of the flesh and hung the rest, cut in thin strips, to dry in the sun. They made a fire, as the Captain had, and roasted some to serve them the next day.

The next morning they found that the flesh in the sun had spoiled, had turned green. They made another fire to cook it to prevent its being wholly lost. For five days they lived on it, not using of their remnant of bread.

They recruited their strength on the flesh, eating it in small pieces with salt water. By the 14th they were able to make a few attempts at guiding the boat with an oar.

On the 15th the flesh was all consumed and they had

left the last of their bread, two sea biscuits. Their limbs
had swelled during the last two days and now began to
pain them excessively. They judged they still had 300
miles to go.

On the 17th the settling of a cloud led Chase to think
that land was near. Notwithstanding, the next morning,
Nickerson, 17 years of age, after having bailed the boat,
lay down, drew a piece of canvas up over him, and said
that he then wished to die immediately. On the 19th, at
7 in the morning, Lawrence saw a sail at seven miles, and
the three of them were taken up by the brig *Indian* of
London, Captain William Crozier.

It is not known what happened in later years to the
three men who survived the island. But the four Nantucket men who, with the Captain, survived the sea, all
became captains themselves. They died old, Nickerson at
77, Ramsdale, who was 19 on the *Essex,* at 75, Chase who
was 24, at 73, Lawrence who was 30, at 80, and Pollard,
the captain, who had been 31 at the time, lived until 1870,
age 81.

The Captain, on his return to Nantucket, took charge of
the ship *Two Brothers,* another whaler, and five months
from home struck a reef to the westward of the Sandwich
Islands. The ship was a total loss, and Pollard never went
to sea again. At the time of the second wreck he said:
"Now I am utterly ruined. No owner will ever trust me
with a whaler again, for all will say I am an unlucky
man." He ended his life as the night watch of Nantucket
town, protecting the houses and people in the dark.

Owen Chase was always fortunate. In 1832 the *Charles
Carrol* was built for him on Brant Point, Nantucket, and
he filled her twice, each time with 2600 barrels of sperm
oil. In his last years he took to hiding food in the attic of
his house.

PART ONE

Call me Ishmael

Call me Ishmael

I take SPACE to be the central fact to man born in America, from Folsom cave to now. I spell it large because it comes large here. Large, and without mercy.

It is geography at bottom, a hell of wide land from the beginning. That made the first American story (Parkman's): exploration.

Something else than a stretch of earth—seas on both sides, no barriers to contain as restless a thing as Western man was becoming in Columbus' day. That made Melville's story (part of it).

PLUS a harshness we still perpetuate, a sun like a tomahawk, small earthquakes but big tornadoes and hurrikans, a river north and south in the middle of the land running out the blood.

The fulcrum of America is the Plains, half sea half land, a high sun as metal and obdurate as the iron horizon, and a man's job to square the circle.

Some men ride on such space, others have to fasten themselves like a tent stake to survive. As I see it Poe dug in and Melville mounted. They are the alternatives.

Americans still fancy themselves such democrats. But their triumphs are of the machine. It is the only master of space the average person ever knows, oxwheel to piston, muscle to jet. It gives trajectory.

To Melville it was not the will to be free but the will to overwhelm nature that lies at the bottom of us as individuals and a people. Ahab is no democrat. Moby-Dick, antagonist, is only king of natural force, resource.

I am interested in a Melville who decided sometime in 1850 to write a book about the whaling industry and what happened to a man in command of one of the most successful machines Americans had perfected up to that time—the whaleship.

This captain, Ahab by name, knew space. He rode it across seven seas. He was an able skipper, what the fishing people I was raised with call a highliner. Big catches: he brought back holds barrel full of the oil of the sperm, the light of American and European communities up to the middle of the 19th century.

This Ahab had gone wild. The object of his attention was something unconscionably big and white. He had become a specialist: he had all space concentrated into the form of a whale called Moby-Dick. And he assailed it as Columbus an ocean, LaSalle a continent, the Donner Party their winter Pass.

I am interested in a Melville who was long-eyed enough

to understand the Pacific as part of our geography, another West, prefigured in the Plains, antithetical.

The beginning of man was salt sea, and the perpetual reverberation of that great ancient fact, constantly renewed in the unfolding of life in every human individual, is the important single fact about Melville. Pelagic.

He had the tradition in him, deep, in his brain, his words, the salt beat of his blood. He had the sea of himself in a vigorous, stricken way, as Poe the street. It enabled him to draw up from Shakespeare. It made Noah, and Moses, contemporary to him. History was ritual and repetition when Melville's imagination was at its own proper beat.

It was an older sense than the European man's, more to do with magic than culture. Magic which, in contrast to worship, is all black. For magic has one purpose: compel men or non-human forces to do one's will. Like Ahab, American, one aim: lordship over nature.

I am willing to ride Melville's image of man, whale and ocean to find in him prophecies, lessons he himself would not have spelled out. A hundred years gives us an advantage. For Melville was as much larger than himself as Ahab's hate. He was a plunger. He knew how to take a chance.

The man made a mess of things. He got all balled up with Christ. He made a white marriage. He had one son die of tuberculosis, the other shoot himself. He only rode his own space once—*Moby-Dick*. He had to be wild or he was nothing in particular. He had to go fast, like an American, or he was all torpor. Half horse half alligator.

Melville took an awful licking. He was bound to. He was an original, aboriginal. A beginner. It happens that way to the dreaming men it takes to discover America: Columbus and LaSalle won, and then lost her to the competent. Daniel Boone loved her earth. Harrod tells the story of coming upon Boone one day far to the west in Kentucky of where Harrod thought any white man had ever been. He heard sound he couldn't place, crept forward to a boulder and there in a blue grass clearing was Boone alone singing to himself. Boone died west of the Mississippi, in his own country criminal—"wanted," a bankrupt of spirit and land.

Beginner—and interested in beginnings. Melville had a way of reaching back through time until he got history pushed back so far he turned time into space. He was like a migrant backtrailing to Asia, some Inca trying to find a lost home.

We are the last "first" people. We forget that. We act big, misuse our land, ourselves. We lose our own primary.

Melville went back, to discover us, to come forward. He got as far as *Moby-Dick*.

Ortega y Gasset puts it that the man of antiquity, before he did anything, took a step like the bullfighter who leaps back in order to deliver the mortal thrust.

Whitman appears, because of his notation of the features of American life and his conscious identification of himself with the people, to be the more poet. But Melville had the will. He was homeless in his land, his society, his self.

Logic and classification had led civilization toward man, away from space. Melville went to space to probe and find man. Early men did the same: poetry, language and the care of myth, as Fenollosa says, grew up together. Among the Egyptians Horus was the god of writing and the god of the moon, one figure for both, a WHITE MONKEY.

In place of Zeus, Odysseus, Olympus we have had Caesar, Faust, the City. The shift was from man as a group to individual man. Now, in spite of the corruption of myth by fascism, the swing is out and back. Melville is one who began it.

He had a pull to the origin of things, the first day, the first man, the unknown sea, Betelgeuse, the buried continent. From passive places his imagination sprang a harpoon.

He sought prime. He had the coldness we have, but he warmed himself by first fires after Flood. It gave him the power to find the lost past of America, the unfound present, and make a myth, *Moby-Dick,* for a people of Ishmaels.

The thing got away from him. It does, from us. We make AHAB, the WHITE WHALE, and lose them. We let John Henry go, Negro, worker, hammering man:

He lied down his hammer an' he died.

Whitman we have called our greatest voice because he gave us hope. Melville is the truer man. He lived intensely his people's wrong, their guilt. But he remembered the first dream. The *White Whale* is more accurate than *Leaves of Grass.* Because it is America, all of her space, the malice, the root.

What lies under

Melville prepared the way for *Moby-Dick* by ridiculing, in 1850, the idea that the literary genius in America would be, like Shakespeare, "a writer of dramas." This was his proposition:

> great geniuses are parts of the times, they themselves are the times, and possess a corresponding colouring.

Melville raised his times up when he got them into *Moby-Dick* and they held firm in his schema:

> e.g. his *crew*, a "people," Clootz and Tom Paine's people, all races and colors functioning together, a forecastle reality of Americans not yet a dream accomplished by the society;

e.g. his *job on the whaling industry,* a problem in
the resolution of forces solved with all forces
taken account of: (1) OWNERS Bildad and Peleg
(Aunt Charity interested party); (2) Ahab, hard
MASTER; (3) the MEN, and TECHNOLOGY,
killer boat, tryworks and underdeck storage of
yield permitting four-year voyage.

We forget the part the chase of the whale played in
American economy. It started from a shortage of fats and
oils. The Indian had no cattle, the colonist not enough.
It was the same with pigs and goats. Red and white alike
had to use substitutes. It accounts for the heavy slaughter
of the passenger pigeon and the curlew, plentiful birds;
and the slaughter of the buffalo.

The Indians appear to have taken shore whales from
an early time. The Makahs around Cape Flattery knew
tricks only the present day Norwegian whalers have ap-
plied. They blew up seal skins to slow the run of a
wounded whale like a sea anchor and to float the dead
whale when heavier than water.

The American Indian continued to be a skilled part of
the industry down to its end, a miserably paid tool. Melville had reason to name his ship *Pequod* and to make the
Gayhead Tashteego one of his three harpooneers.

COMBUSTION. All whales yield oil. Most of the oil
is a true fat, a glyceride of the fatty acids. Unlike the
Indians the settlers did not find it edible. They boiled
the blubber down for tallow. In addition *to* this fat, com-
monly called whale oil, the sperm whale and the bottle-
nose yield a solid wax called spermaceti and a liquid wax
called sperm oil. The spermaceti wax is contained in the
cavity of the head (vide chp. CISTERN AND BUCKETS, *Moby-
Dick*), and in the bones.

Economic historians, lubbers, fail to heft the industry in American economic life up to the Civil War. (In 1859 petroleum was discovered in Pennsylvania. Kerosene, petroleum, and paraffin began rapidly to replace whale oil, sperm oil, and spermaceti wax as illuminating oil, lubricants, and raw materials for candles.)

Whaling expanded at a time when agriculture not industry was the base of labor and when foreign not domestic commerce was the base of trade. A few facts:

> by 1833, 70,000 persons and $70,000,000 were tied up in whaling and such associated crafts as shipbuilding, sail-lofts, smiths to make toggle irons, the thieving outfitters, their agents and the whores of ports like New Bedford;

> by 1844 (peak years roughly 1840-1860) the figure is up to $120,000,000, whaling competes successfully in attracting capital to itself with such opening industries as textiles and shoes, and the export of whale products—one-fourth of the catch—is third to meat products and lumber.

A NECESSARY DISSOCIATION: the notion that the China trade and clipper ships made and made up the maritime America which went down as did agrarian America before land and finance speculation, hard metal industry.

The China trade was, economically, distribution, appeared after England closed the West Indies to our rum merchants following the Revolution. It was the way the smugglers, themselves the answer to England's pre-Revolutionary restrictions, went straight.

Whaling was production, as old as the colonies and, in capital and function, forerunner to a later America, with more relation to Socony than to clippers and the China trade.

As early as 1688 there is a record at Boston of a New York brig petitioning Governor Andross for permission to set out "upon a fishing design about the Bohames Islands, And Cap florida, for sperma Coeti whales and Racks."

This was new to whaling, BRAND NEW, American. A FIRST. All the way back to French and Spanish Basques of the Middle Ages it had been cold water whales, the black, right or Greenland whales of northern waters, which had been hunted. But the Yankees had discovered that the Sperm whale had the finest oil and brought the biggest price.

They went after it. And it led them into all the oceans. And gave whaling its leading role in making the Pacific the American lake the navy now, after a lapse of 100 years, has been about the business of certifying.

A FACT: whale logbooks are today furnishing sea lawyers first claims to islands—the flag & all that;

for whaler as pioneer, cf. chp. THE ADVOCATE, *Moby-Dick*.

You will also discover in that chapter Melville's figures on the value of the industry. Compare to mine above. Thus:

we whalemen of America now outnumber all the rest of the banded whalemen in the world; sail a navy of upward of seven hundred vessels; manned by eighteen thousand men; yearly consuming 4,000,000 dollars; the ships worth, at the time of sailing, $20,000,000; and every year reporting into our harbours a well-reaped harvest of $7,000,000.

About this outnumbering: of 900 whaling vessels of all nations in 1846, 735 were American.

All this is by way of CORRECTION. I don't intend to
dish up cold pork. There are histories of whaling if you
are interested. BUT no study weighs the industry in the
scale of the total society. What you get is this: many of
the earliest industrial fortunes were built on the "bless-
ing" of the whale fishery!

TWO INTERPOLATIONS. Melville did not know
Number 1. Maybe somewhere he does point out Number
2. For he was wide. Add to his knowledge of whaling:

merchant marine	(read *Redburn*)
the Navy	(ditto *White-Jacket*)
assorted carriers of the Pacific	(*Omoo, Mardi,* etc.)
and the Spanish	(by all means read "Benito Cereno" and "The En-cantadas," the finest things outside *Moby-Dick*)

Interpolation 1

1762: the colonies still very English, so much so they have
   little to do with one another, face and act toward London.

Rhode Island: makers of spermaceti candles meet and
   make covenant to raise the price of wax candles—and
   keep it raised, it goes without saying. The first American TRUST.

Name: The United Company of Spermaceti Chandlers.

Importance: "shows how colonial boundaries were being
   eliminated in the minds of the moneyed groups as con-
   trasted with the as yet extremely provincial outlook and
   provincial patriotism of the smaller people of town and
   country."

I'm putting a stress Melville didn't on whaling as

industry. Cutting out the glory: a book *Moby-Dick* turns out to be its glory. We still are soft about our industries, wonder-eyed. What's important is the energy they are a clue to, the drive in the people. The things made are OK, too, some of them. But the captains of industry ain't worth the powder etc. Take the Revolution so long as we're on the subject: whose revolution was it but the "moneyed groups'"; Breed's Hill two weeks after Lexington and it was all over for the "smaller people" until Jefferson gave them another chance.

Don't think whaling was any different from any other American industry. The first men in it, the leaders, explorers, were WORKERS. The money and the glory came later, on top with the exploiters. And the force went down, stayed where it always does, at the underpaid bottom. Where the worker is after the leader is gone.

Whaling started, like so many American industries, as a collective, communal affair. See any history of Sag Harbor or Nantucket. And as late as 1850 there were still skippers to remember the days when they knew the fathers of every man in their crew. But it was already a sweated industry by the time Melville was a hand on a lay (1841-43).

THE TRICK—then as now:

> reduce labor costs lower than worker's efficiency—during the 1840's and '50's it cost the owners 15¢ to 30¢ a day to feed each crew member

> combine inefficient workers and such costs by maintaining lowest wages and miserable working conditions—vide TYPEE, early chps., and *Omoo*, same.

THE RESULT: by the 1840's the crews were the bottom dogs of all nations and all races. Of the 18,000 men (Melville above) *one-half* ranked as green hands and more than *two-thirds* deserted every voyage.

There were so many Pacific natives like Queequeg, the second colored harpooneer, that a section of Nantucket came to be known as New Guinea.

There were so many Portuguese from the Islands that a section of New Bedford was called Fayal.

The third of Melville's harpooneers was the imperial African Negro Ahasuerus Daggoo.

For bottom dogs made pretty SEE the balletic chapter called MIDNIGHT, FORECASTLE, in *Moby-Dick*.

I insert here a document of our history left out of the published works of Herman Melville. It was written at the same time as *Moby-Dick* and is headed:

> *"What became of the ship's company of the whaleship 'Acushnet,' according to Hubbard who came home in her (more than a four years' voyage) and who visited me at Pittsfield in 1850."*

Captain Pease—retired & lives ashore at the Vineyard
Raymond 1st Mate—had a fight with the Captain & went ashore at Payta
Hall 2nd Mate came home & went to California
3rd Mate, Portuguese, went ashore at Payta
Boatsteerer Brown, Portuguese, either ran away or killed at Ropo one of the Marquesas
Smith went ashore at Santa coast of Peru, afterwards committed suicide at Mobile
Barney boatsteerer came home
Carpenter went ashore at Mowee half dead with disreputable disease

The Crew:
Tom Johnson, black, went ashore at Mowee half dead (ditto) & died at the hospital
Reed—mulatto—came home

Blacksmith—ran away at St. Francisco
Backus—little black—Do
Bill Green—after various attempts at running away, came
  home in the end
The Irishman ran away at Salango, coast of Columbia
Wright went ashore half dead at the Marquesas
John Adams & Jo Portuguese came home
The old cook came home
Haynes ran away aboard of a Sydney ship
Little Jack—came home
Grant—young fellow—went ashore half dead, spitting
  blood, at Oahu
Murray went ashore, shunning fight, at Rio Janeiro
The Cooper—came home

Melville himself is a case in point. He deserted the
Acushnet, his first whaleship, at the Marquesas. He was
one of eleven mutineers aboard his second, a Sydney ship
the *Lucy Ann,* at Tahiti. Nothing is known of his con-
duct on the third, except that he turned up after it,
ashore, at Honolulu.

So if you want to know why Melville nailed us in *Moby-
Dick,* consider whaling. Consider whaling as FRON-
TIER, and INDUSTRY. A product wanted, men got it:
big business. The Pacific as sweatshop. Man, led, against
the biggest damndest creature nature uncorks. The whaleship as factory, the whaleboat the precision instrument.
The 1840's: the New West in the saddle and Melville
No. 20 of a rough and bastard crew. Are they the essen-
tials?

BIG? Melville may never have seen the biggest of
whales, the blue, the principal kill of the present day. He
reaches his full size, 100 feet, at 11 years, lives 20 to 25
years, and weighs 150 tons—or four times the estimated

weight of the biggest prehistoric monster and equal to the weight of 37 elephants or 150 fat oxen.

There are two classes of whale: the baleen and the toothed whale. The blue is a baleen. Melville was satisfied with the biggest of the toothed whales, the sperm.

Whales have lungs. To breathe they come to the surface about every half hour. It is this fact that makes them vulnerable to attack by the only important enemy they have—the whaleman.

Melville didn't put it all on the surface of *Moby-Dick*. You'll find the frontier all right, and Andrew Jackson regarded as heavyweight champion (READ end of first KNIGHTS AND SQUIRES chapter for finest rhetoric of democracy). And the technic of an industry analyzed, scrupulously described. But no economics. Jefferson and John Adams observed that in their young days very few men had thought about "government," there were very few writers on "government." Yes, the year *Moby-Dick* was being finished Marx was writing letters to the N. Y. *Daily Tribune*. But Melville . . . . . .

SOME NECESSARY ECOLOGY. With his baleen the blue whale strains out of the water and eats KRILL. Krill is a shrimplike fish which itself feeds on floating green diatoms. These algae develop in summer in the neighborhood of drift ice.

> *color:* krill spawn at the border of arctic and antarctic ice. The offspring drift with the currents toward the equator. They are in such abundance they turn the waters pink.

The sperm whale feeds on cuttlefish, particularly on the GIANT SQUID which grows to a 33-foot spread of tentacles and an arm length of 21 feet. Compare *Moby-*

Dick, LIX, SQUID. The squid lives on big prawn and small fish, and to catch him the whale dives into depths of several hundred fathom. The struggle leaves sores and marks of the armed suckers on the whale's skin around the mouth.

. . . . . . what counts, Melville had, the *experience,* what lies under. And his own *force* to resolve the forces.

Interpolation No. 2

Quote. The American whaling era—in contrast to the
Basque, French, Dutch and English—
developed independently
concentrated on different species of whale
covered all seas including the Arctic
yielded on a larger scale than in any other country or group of countries before.

Unquote.

Usufruct

1841

Jan.-June

"When I was on board the ship Acush-net of Fairhaven, on the passage to the Pacific cruising-grounds, among other matters of forecastle conversations at times was the story of the Essex. It was then that I first became acquainted with her history and her truly astounding fate.

"But what then served to specialize my interest at the time was the circumstance that the Second mate of our ship, Mr Hall, an Englishman & Londoner by birth, had for two three-years voyages sailed with Owen Chace (then in command of the whaleship "Charles Carroll" of Nantucket). This Hall always spoke of Chace with much interest & sincere regard—but he did not seem to know anything more about him or the Essex affair than any body else.

December

"Somewhere about the latter part of A.D. 1841, in this same ship the Acushnet, we spoke the "Charles Carroll" of Nantucket, & Owen Chace was the captain, & so it came to pass that I saw him. He was a large, powerful well-made man; rather tall; to all appearances something past forty-five or so; with a handsome face for a Yankee, & expressive of great uprightness & calm unostentatious courage. His whole appearance impressed me pleasurably. He was the most prepossessing-looking whalehunter I think I ever saw.

"Being a mere foremast-hand I had no opportunity of conversing with Owen (tho' he was on board our ship for two hours at a time) nor have I ever seen him since.

November

"But I should have before mentioned, that before seeing Chace's ship, we spoke another Nantucket craft & *gammed* with her. In the forecastle I made the acquaintance of a fine lad of sixteen or thereabouts, a son of Owen Chace! I

questioned him concerning his father's
adventure; and when I left his ship to
return again the next morning (for the
two vessels were to sail in company for
a few days) he went to his chest &
handed me a complete copy (same edi-
tion as this one) of the Narrative. This
was the first printed account of it I had
ever seen, & the only copy of Chace's
Narrative (regular & authentic) except
the present one.

"The reading of this wondrous story
upon the landless sea, & close to the very
latitude of the shipwreck had a surprising effect upon me."

All the above—under the heading *"What I Know of Owen
Chace, &c"*—is written in Melville's own copy of

NARRATIVE OF THE MOST
EXTRAORDINARY AND DIS-
TRESSING SHIPWRECK OF THE
WHALE-SHIP ESSEX, OF NAN-
TUCKET; WHICH WAS AT-
TACKED AND FINALLY DE-
STROYED BY A LARGE SPERMA-
CETI-WHALE, IN THE PACIFIC
OCEAN. By OWEN CHASE, of
NANTUCKET, First Mate of Said
Vessel. LONDON, 1821.

1851

The comments by Melville appear to
have been written in the spring of 1851.
Melville at that time was already a year
out on the writing of *Moby-Dick* and
was approaching the end, preparing to

close with the destruction by the White Whale of the ship *Pequod,* the three-day catastrophe which parallels what happened to the *Essex.*

The front fly-leaf carries this inscription in Melville's hand:

Herman Melville from Judge Shaw, April, 1851. The Chief Justice, his father-in-law, had acquired the copy for Melville a month earlier from Thomas Macy at Nantucket.*

April

"*General Evidence*

"This thing of the Essex is found (stupidly alterated) in many compilations of nautical adventure made within the last 15 or 20 years.

"The Englishman Bennett in his exact work *(Whaling Voyage Round the Globe)* quotes the thing as an acknowledged fact.

"Besides seamen, some landsmen (Judge Shaw & others) acquainted with Nantucket, have evinced to me their unquestioning faith in the thing; having seen Captain Pollard himself, & being conversant with his situation in Nantucket since the disaster.

"*Authorship of the Book*

"There seems no reason to suppose

---

* I publish these notes for the first time through the courtesy of the present owner of the volume, Mr. Perc Brown.

I have raised questions about the *Essex,* as well as on the *Acushnet* and the *Globe,* with friends Tripp of New Bedford and Stackpole of Nantucket, and they have been most kind. As were Dr. and Mrs. Will Gardner when I was last on the Island.

that Owen himself wrote the narrative. It bears obvious tokens of having been written for him; but at the same time, its whole air plainly evinces that it was carefully & conscientiously written to Owen's dictation of the facts.—It is almost as good as tho' Owen wrote it himself.

"Another Narrative of the Adventure
"I have been told that Pollard, the Captain, wrote, or caused to be wrote under his own name, his version of the story. I have seen extracts purporting to be from some such work. But I have never seen the work itself. —I should imagine Owen Chace to have been the fittest person to narrate the thing."

In Melville's copy the last pages of the Narrative are missing. So he adds in his notes—under the title *"Sequel"*—a summary of what happened to the "poor fellows" in the Captain's boat and what he had learned of the fate of the three men left on Elizabeth Isle. He records how Pollard fetched his next command up on unknown rocks off the Sandwich Islands, disclosing that "I got this from Hall, Second Mate of the Acushnet." Melville goes on:

"Pollard, it seems, now took the hint, & after reaching home from the second shipwreck, moved to abide ashore. He has ever since lived in Nantucket. Hall told me that he became a butcher there. I believe he is still living."

At this point he makes a general comment:

> "All the sufferings of these miserable
> men of the Essex might, in all human
> probability, have been avoided had they,
> immediately after leaving the wreck,
> steered straight for Tahiti, from which
> they were not very distant at the time
> and *to* which there was a fair trade wind.
> But they dreaded cannibals & strange to
> tell knew not that for more than 20
> years the English missions had been resi-
> dent in Tahiti, & that in the same year
> of the shipwreck—1820—it was entirely
> safe for the ships to touch at Tahiti. But
> they chose to stem a head wind & make
> a passage of some thousand miles (an
> unavoidably roundabout one, too) in
> order to gain a civilized harbour on the
> coast of South America."

He continues with remarks *"Further Concerning Owen
Chace"*:

> "The miserable pertinaciousness of mis-
> fortune which pursued Pollard, the
> Captain, in his second disaster & entire
> shipwreck, did likewise hunt poor
> Owen, tho' somewhat more dilatory in
> overtaking him, the second time.

> "For, while I was in the Acushnet we
> heard from some whaleship that we
> spoke, that the captain of the "Charles
> Carroll"—that is Owen Chace—had re-
> cently received letters from home, in-
> forming him of the certain infidelity of

his wife, the mother of several children, one of them being the lad of sixteen, whom I alluded to as giving me a copy of his father's narrative to read. We also heard that this receipt of this news had told most heavily upon Chace, & that he was a prey to the deepest gloom."

There is a last note, without a heading. It reads:

probably
July, 1852

"Since writing the foregoing I—sometime about 1850-3—saw Capt. Pollard on the island of Nantucket, and exchanged some words with him. To the islanders he was a nobody—to me, the most impressive man, tho' wholly unassuming, even humble, that I ever encountered."

And added, in pencil, along the margin of his earlier remarks concerning Pollard, this:

"a night-watchman"

PART TWO

Shakespeare

Which is the best of Shakespeare's plays?
I mean in what mood and with what ac-
companiment do you like the sea best?"

KEATS, *Letter to Jane Reynolds*
Sept. 14, 1817

Shakespeare, or the discovery of Moby-Dick

Moby-Dick was two books written between February, 1850 and August, 1851.

The first book did not contain Ahab.

It may not, except incidentally, have contained Moby-Dick.

On the 7th of August, 1850, the editor Evert Duyckinck reported to his brother:

> Melville has a new book mostly done, a romantic, fanciful & most literal & most enjoyable presentment of the Whale Fishery—something quite new.

It is not surprising that Melville turned to whaling in

February, 1850, on his return from a trip to England to sell his previous book, *White-Jacket*. It was the last of the materials his sea experience offered him.

He had used his adventures among the South Sea islands in *Typee* (1846) and *Omoo* (1847). He had gone further in the vast archipelago of *Mardi,* written in 1847 and 1848, to map the outlines of his vision of life. The books of 1849, *Redburn* and *White-Jacket,* he had based on his experiences aboard a merchant ship and a man-of-war. The whaling voyage in the *Acushnet* was left.

There is no evidence that Melville had decided on the subject before he started to write in February. On the contrary. Melville's reading is a gauge of him, at all points of his life. He was a skald, and knew how to appropriate the work of others. He read to write. Highborn stealth, Edward Dahlberg calls originality, the act of a cutpurse Autolycus who makes his thefts as invisible as possible. Melville's books batten on other men's books. Yet he bought no books on whaling among the many volumes purchased in England on his trip and soon after his return Putnam's the publishers were picking up in London for him such things as Thomas Beale's *The Natural History of the Sperm Whale.*

He went at it as he had his last two books, "two jobs," as he called *Redburn* and *White-Jacket* in a letter to his father-in-law, "which I have done for money—being forced to it, as other men are to sawing wood." He had a family to support.

By May it was half done. So he told Richard Henry Dana in a letter on the 1st, the only other information of the first Moby-Dick which has survived. The book was giving Melville trouble. Referring to it as "the 'whaling voyage,'" he writes:

> It will be a strange sort of a book, I fear; blubber is blubber you know; tho you may get oil out of it,

the poetry runs as hard as sap from a frozen maple tree;—& to cook the thing up, one must needs throw in a little fancy, which from the nature of the thing, must be ungainly as the gambols of the whales themselves. Yet I mean to give the truth of the thing, spite of this.

That's the record of Moby-Dick No. 1, as it stands. There is nothing on why, in the summer of 1850, Melville changed his conception of the work and, on something "mostly done" on August 7th, spent another full year until, in August, 1851, he had created what we know as *Moby-Dick or, The Whale.*

"Dollars damn me." Melville had the bitter thing of men of originality, the struggle between money and me. It was on him, hard, in the spring of 1850. He says as much in the Dana letter: "I write these books of mine almost entirely for 'lucre'—by the job, as a wood-sawyer saws wood," repeating on Moby-Dick what he had said about *Redburn* and *White-Jacket.*

He knew the cost if he let his imagination loose. He had taken his head once, with *Mardi.* In this new work on whaling he felt obliged, as he had, after *Mardi,* with *Redburn* and *White-Jacket,* "to refrain from writing the kind of book I would wish to."

He would give the truth of the thing, spite of this, yes. His head was lifted to Dana as it was to his father-in-law seven months earlier. He did his work clean. *Exs: Redburn* and *White-Jacket.* "In writing these two books I have not repressed myself much—so far as *they* are concerned; but have spoken pretty much as I feel."

There was only one thing in the spring of 1850 which he did not feel he could afford to do: "So far as I am individually concerned, & independent of my pocket, it is my earnest desire to write those sort of books which are said to 'fail.' "

In the end, in *Moby-Dick,* he did. Within three months he took his head again. Why?

Through May he continued to try to do a quick book for the market: "all my books are botches." Into June he fought his materials: "blubber is blubber." Then something happened. What, Melville tells:

> I somehow cling to the strange fancy, that, in all men hiddenly reside certain wondrous, occult properties —as in some plants and minerals—which by some happy but very rare accident (as bronze was discovered by the melting of the iron and brass at the burning of Corinth) may chance to be called forth here on earth.

When? Melville is his own tell-tale: he wrote these words in July, 1850. They occur in an article he did for Duyckinck's magazine. He gave it the title HAWTHORNE AND HIS MOSSES, WRITTEN BY A VIRGINIAN SPENDING A JULY IN VERMONT.

The subject is Hawthorne, Shakespeare and Herman Melville. It is a document of Melville's rights and perceptions, his declaration of the freedom of a man to fail. Within a matter of days after it was written (July 18 ff.), Melville had abandoned the account of the Whale Fishery and gambled it and himself with Ahab and the White Whale.

The *Mosses* piece is a deep and lovely thing. The spirit is asweep, as in the book to come. The confusion of May is gone. Melville is charged again. *Moby-Dick* is already shadowed in the excitement over genius, and America as a subject for genius. You can feel Ahab in the making,

Ahab of "the globular brain and ponderous heart," so much does Melville concern himself with the distinction between the head and the heart in Hawthorne and Shakespeare. You can see the prose stepping off.

The germinous seeds Hawthorne has dropped in Melville's July soil begin to grow: Bulkington, the secret member of the crew in *Moby-Dick*, is here, hidden, in what Melville quotes as Hawthorne's self-portrait—the "seeker," rough-hewn and brawny, of large, warm heart and powerful intellect.

Above all, in the ferment, Shakespeare, the cause. The passages on him—the manner in which he is introduced, the detail with which he is used, the intensity—tell the story of what had happened. Melville had read him again. His copy of THE PLAYS survives. He had bought it in Boston in February, 1849. He described it then to Duyckinck:

> It is an edition in glorious great type, every letter whereof is a soldier, & the top of every 't' like a musket barrel.
>
> I am mad to think how minute a cause has prevented me hitherto from reading Shakespeare. But until now any copy that was come-atable to me happened to be a vile small print unendurable to my eyes which are tender as young sperms.
>
> But chancing to fall in with this glorious edition, I now exult over it, page after page.

The set exists, seven volumes, with passages marked, and comments in Melville's hand. The significant thing is the rough notes for the composition of *Moby-Dick* on the fly-leaf of the last volume. These notes involve Ahab, Pip, Bulkington, Ishmael, and are the key to Melville's intention with these characters. They thus relate not to what we know of the Moby-Dick that Melville had been working on up to July but to *Moby-Dick* as he came to conceive it at this time.

Joined to the passages on Shakespeare in the *Mosses* piece, the notes in the Shakespeare set verify what *Moby-Dick* proves: Melville and Shakespeare had made a Corinth and out of the burning came *Moby-Dick,* bronze.

A note of thanks

The Melville people are rare people, and this is the right place to tell:

of Eleanor Melville Metcalf and Henry K. Metcalf, with whom the Shakespeare was only a beginning, for they have made all Melville's things mine, indeed have made me a member of their family;

of Raymond Weaver and Henry A. Murray, Jr., the other true biographer, who have been my generous friends;

and of those early criers of Melville, Carl Van Doren and Van Wyck Brooks, who have spoken up for me.

For the original use of the Shakespeare set and Melville's notes in it I wish also to thank another granddaughter, Mrs. Frances Osborne.

American Shiloh

Shakespeare emerged from the first rush of Melville's reading a Messiah: as he put it in the *Mosses* piece in 1850, a "Shiloh"; as he put it to Duyckinck in 1849, "full of sermons-on-the-mount, and gentle, aye, almost as Jesus." Melville had a way of ascribing divinity to truth-tellers, Solomon, Shakespeare, Hawthorne, or Jesus.

He next limited Shakespeare. He advanced a criticism in his second letter to Duyckinck in 1849 which is central to all his later published passages on the poet. It keeps him this side idolatry. It arises from what Melville takes to be an "American" advantage:

> I would to God Shakespeare had lived later, & prom- enaded in Broadway. Not that I might have had the

pleasure of leaving my card for him at the Astor, or made merry with him over a bowl of the fine Duyck-inck punch; but that the muzzle which all men wore on their souls in the Elizabethan day, might not have intercepted Shakespeare's free articulations, for I hold it a verity, that even Shakespeare was not a frank man to the uttermost. And, indeed, who in this intolerant universe is, or can be? But the Declaration of Independence makes a difference.

In the *Mosses* piece, a year and a half later, he gives it tone:

In Shakespeare's tomb lies infinitely more than Shakespeare ever wrote. And if I magnify Shakes-peare, it is not so much for what he did do as for what he did not do, or refrained from doing.

For in this world of lies, Truth is forced to fly like a scared white doe in the woodlands; and only by cun-ning glimpses will she reveal herself, as in Shakes-peare and other masters of the great Art of Telling the Truth,—even though it be covertly and by snatches.

In his copy of the PLAYS, when Shakespeare muzzles truth-speakers, Melville is quick to mark the line or inci-dent. In *Antony and Cleopatra* he puts a check beside Enobarbus' blunt answer to Antony's correction of his speech: "That truth should be silent I had almost forgot."

In *Lear* he underscores the Fool's answer to Lear's angry threat of the whip: "Truth's a dog must to kennel; he must be whipp'd out, when Lady the brach may stand by th' fire and stink." The very language of Melville in the *Mosses* thing is heard from the Fool's mouth.

As an artist Melville chafed at representation. His work up to *Moby-Dick* was a progress toward the concrete and after *Moby-Dick* a breaking away. He had to fight himself to give truth dramatic location. Shakespeare's dramatic significance was not lost upon him, but he would have been, as he says, "more content with the still, rich utterance of a great intellect in repose." Melville's demand uncovers a flaw in himself.

Fortunately—for *Moby-Dick*—the big truth was not sermons-on-the-mount. Melville found these in *Measure for Measure*. It is, rather

> those deep far-away things in him; those occasional flashings-forth of the intuitive Truth in him; those short, quick probings at the very axis of reality;—these are the things that make Shakespeare, Shakespeare.

Such reality is in the mouths of the "dark" characters, Hamlet, Timon, Lear and Iago, where the drama Melville could learn from, lay. For blackness fixed and fascinated Melville. Through such dark men Shakespeare

> craftily says, or sometimes insinuates the things which we feel to be so terrifically true, that it were all but madness for any good man, in his own proper character, to utter or even hint of them!

It is this side of Shakespeare that Melville fastens on. Madness, villainy and evil are called up out of the plays as though Melville's pencil were a wand of black magic. To use Swinburne's comment on *Lear*, it is not the light of revelation but the darkness of it that Melville finds most profound in Shakespeare. He was to write in *Moby-Dick*:

> Though in many of its aspects the visible world seems formed in love, the invisible spheres were formed in fright.

Man, to man

Shakespeare reflects Melville's disillusion in the treacherous world. In *The Tempest,* when Miranda cries out "O brave new world!", Melville encircles Prospero's answer " 'Tis new to thee," and writes this note at the bottom of the page:

> Consider the character of the persons concerning whom Miranda says this—then Prospero's quiet words in comment—how terrible! In *Timon* itself there is nothing like it.

Shakespeare frequently expresses disillusion through friendship and its falling off. The theme has many variations. Melville misses none of them. Caesar and Antony on the fickleness of the people to their rulers, in *Antony and Cleopatra*. Achilles and Ulysses on the people's faithlessness to their heroes, in *Troilus* and *Cressida*. Henry V and Richard II on treachery within the councils of the state. Melville pulls it out of the tragedies: in *Lear*, when the Fool sings how fathers who bear bags draw forth love and those who wear rags lose love; and in *Hamlet*, the lines of the Player King:

> For who not needs, shall never lack a friend
> And who in want a hollow friend doth try,
> Directly seasons him his enemy.

To betray a friend was to make—for Melville as for Richard—a second fall of cursed man. Shakespeare gives the theme its great counterpoint in *Timon*. In that play the whole issue of idealism is objectified through friendship. When his friends fail him Timon's love turns to hate. His world—and with it the play—wrenches into halves as the earth with one lunge tore off from a sun.

Melville took a more personal possession of the tragedy of Timon than of any of the other dark men. In *Lear* he found ingratitude, but what gave *Timon* its special intensity was that Timon was undone by friends, not daughters.

Melville makes little out of the love of man and woman. It is the friendship of men which is love. That is why Hawthorne was so important to him, to whom he wrote his best letters and to whom he dedicated *Moby-Dick*. That is why he never forgot Jack Chase, the handsome sailor he worked under in the Pacific, to whom he dedicated his last book, *Billy Budd*.

Melville had the Greek sense of men's love. Or the Roman's, as Shakespeare gives it in *Coriolanus*. In that play the only place Melville heavily marks is the long passage in which Coriolanus and Aufidius meet and em-

brace. They are captains, with the soldier's sense of com-
rade. Melville's is the seaman's, of a shipmate. Aufidius
speaks the same passionate images of friendship Melville
uses to convey the depth of feeling between Ishmael and
Queequeg in *Moby-Dick*. Ishmael and Queequeg are as
"married" as Aufidius feels toward Coriolanus:

> that I see thee here
> Thou noble thing, more dances my rapt heart
> Than when I first my wedded mistress saw
> Bestride my threshold.

Like Timon Melville found only disappointment. He
lost Jack Chase, and Hawthorne, shyest grape, hid from
him. In a poem of his later years Melville wrote:

> To have known him, to have loved him
>   After loneness long
> And then to be estranged in life
>   And neither in the wrong
> Ease me, a little ease, my song!

Timon is mocked with glory, as his faithful Steward
says, lives, as Melville notes, but in a dream of friendship.
Melville uses the blasted hero as a symbol throughout his
books, sometimes in Plutarch's convention as a misan-
thrope, often as another Ishmael of solitude, most signifi-
cantly—in *Pierre*—as disillusion itself, man undone by
goodness. It is the subject of *Pierre* and the lesson of *The
Confidence Man*.

Melville's feeling for the play is summarized by a line
he underscores in it, the Stranger's observation on the
hypocrisy of Timon's friends:

> Why, this is the world's soul.

Lear and Moby-Dick

It was *Lear* that had the deep creative impact. In *Moby-Dick* the use is pervasive. That its use is also the most implicit of any play serves merely to enforce a law of the imagination, for what has stirred Melville's own most is heaved out, like Cordelia's heart, with most tardiness.

In the Hawthorne-Mosses article it is to Lear's speeches that Melville points to prove Shakespeare's insinuations of "the things we feel to be so terrifically true:"

> Tormented into desperation, Lear, the frantic king, tears off the mask, and speaks the same madness of vital truth.

Under this title an earlier version of this material appeared in the magazine *Twice-A-Year*.

His copy of the play is marked more heavily than any of
the others but *Antony and Cleopatra*. Of the characters
the Fool and Edmund receive the attention. I have said
Melville found his own words in the Fool's mouth when
the Fool cries, "Truth's a dog must to kennel." He found
them in such other speeches of that boy, as

> Nay, an thou canst not smile as the wind sits, thou'lt
> catch cold shortly.

For Melville sees the Fool as the Shakespeare he would
have liked more of, not one who refrained from hinting
what he knew.

Melville is terrified by Edmund who took his fierce
quality in the lusty stealth of nature and who, in his evil,
leagued with that world whose thick rotundity Lear
would strike flat. The sources of this man's evil, and his
qualities, attract the writer who is likewise drawn to
Goneril, to Iago—and who himself creates a Jackson in
Redburn and a Claggart in *Billy Budd*.

It is the positive qualities in the depraved: Edmund's
courage, and his power of attracting love. When Edmund
outfaces Albany's challenge, denies he is a traitor, and
insists he will firmly prove his truth and honor, Melville
writes this footnote:

> The infernal nature has a valor often denied to
> innocence.

When Edmund is dying he fails to revoke his order for
the death of Lear and Cordelia, only looks upon the bodies
of Goneril and Regan and consoles himself: "Yet Edmund
was belov'd!" This Melville heavily checks. It is a twisting
ambiguity like one of his own—Evil beloved.

Melville is dumb with horror at the close, blood-stop
double meaning of Shakespeare's language in the scene of

the blinding of Gloucester. His comment is an exclamation: "Terrific!" When Regan calls Gloucester "Ingrateful fox!" Melville writes:

> Here's a touch Shakespearean—*Regan* talks of *ingratitude!*

First causes were Melville's peculiar preoccupation. He concentrates on an Edmund, a Regan—and the world of *Lear*, which is almost generated by such creatures, lies directly behind the creation of an Ahab, a Fedallah and the White, lovely, monstrous Whale.

Melville found answers in the darkness of *Lear*. Not in the weak goodness of an Albany who thinks to exclude evil from good by a remark as neat and corrective as Eliphaz in the Book of Job:

> Wisdom and goodness to the vile seem vile;
> Filths savor but themselves.

The ambiguities do not resolve themselves by such "right-mindedness." Albany is a Starbuck.

Melville turned rather to men who suffered as Job suffered—to Lear and Edgar and Gloucester. Judged by his markings upon the scene in which Edgar discovers, with a hot burst in his heart, his father's blindness, Melville perceived what suggests itself as a symbol so inherent to the play as to leave one amazed it has not been more often observed—that to lose the eye and capacity to see, to lose the physical organ, "vile jelly," is to gain spiritual sight.

The crucifixion in *Lear* is not of the limbs on a cross-beam, but of the eyes put out, the eyes of pride too sharp for feeling. Lear himself in the storm scene senses it, but Gloucester blind speaks it: "I stumbled when I saw."

Lear's words:

Poor naked wretches, wheresoe'er you are,
That bide the pelting of this pitiless storm,
How shall your houseless heads and unfed sides,
Your loop'd and window'd raggedness, defend you
From seasons such as these? O, I have ta'en
Too little care of this! Take physic, pomp;
Expose thyself to feel what wretches feel,
That thou mayst shake the superflux to them
And show the heavens more just.

Gloucester's words come later, Act IV, Sc. 1. It is the purgatorial dispensation of the whole play. Gloucester, who aches to have his son Edgar back—

Might I but live to *see thee in my touch,*
I'ld say I had eyes again!

—has his wish and does not know it. He does not know, because he cannot see, that Edgar is already there beside him in the disguise of Tom o' Bedlam. Gloucester takes him for the poor, mad beggar he says he is. He seconds Lear thus:

Here, take this purse, thou whom the heavens'
     plagues
Have humbled to all strokes. That I am wretched
Makes thee the happier. Heavens, deal so still!
Let the superfluous and lust-dieted man,
That slaves your ordinance, that will not see
Because he does not feel, feel your pow'r quickly;
So distribution should undo excess,
And each man have enough.

The underscore is Melville's.

What moves Melville is the stricken goodness of a Lear, a Gloucester, an Edgar, who in suffering feel and thus probe more closely to the truth. Melville is to put Ahab through this humbling.

Shakespeare drew *Lear* out of what Melville called "the infinite obscure of his background." It was most kin to Melville. He uses it as an immediate obscure around his own world of *Moby-Dick*. And he leaves Ishmael at the end to tell the tale of Ahab's tragedy as Kent remained to speak these last words of Lear:

> Vex not his ghost. O, let him pass! He hates him
> That would upon the rack of this tough world
> Stretch him out longer.

A Moby-Dick manuscript

It is beautifully right to find what I take to be rough
notes for *Moby-Dick* in the Shakespeare set itself. They
are written in Melville's hand, in pencil, upon the last
fly-leaf of the last volume, the one containing *Lear,
Othello* and *Hamlet*. I transcribe them as they stand:

Ego non baptizo te in nomine Patris et
Filii et Spiritus Sancti—sed in nomine
Diaboli. —madness is undefinable—
It & right reason extremes of one,
—not the (black art) Goetic but Theurgic magic—
seeks converse with the Intelligence, Power, the
Angel.

The Latin is a longer form of what Melville told Hawthorne to be the secret motto of *Moby-Dick*. In the novel Ahab howls it as an inverted benediction upon the harpoon he has tempered in savage blood:

> Ego non baptizo te in nomine patris, sed in nomine diaboli.

> I do not baptize thee in the name of the father, but in the name of the devil.

The change in the wording from the notes to the novel is of extreme significance. It is not for economy of phrase. The removal of Christ and the Holy Ghost—Filii et Spiritus Sancti—is a mechanical act mirroring the imaginative. Of necessity, from Ahab's world, both Christ and the Holy Ghost are absent. Ahab moves and has his being in a world to which They and what They import are inimical: remember, Ahab fought a deadly scrimmage with a Spaniard before the altar at Santa, and spat into the silver calabash. The conflict in Ahab's world is abrupt, more that between Satan and Jehovah, of the old dispensation than the new. It is the outward symbol of the inner truth that the name of Christ is uttered but once in the book and then it is torn from Starbuck, the only possible man to use it, at a moment of anguish, the night before the fatal third day of the chase.

Ahab is Conjur Man. He invokes his own evil world. He himself uses black magic to achieve his vengeful ends. With the very words "in nomine diaboli" he believes he utters a Spell and performs a Rite of such magic.

The Ahab-world is closer to *Macbeth* than to *Lear*. In it the supernatural is accepted. Fedallah appears as freely as the Weird Sisters. Before Ahab's first entrance he has reached that identification with evil to which Macbeth out of fear evolves within the play itself. The agents of evil give both Ahab and Macbeth a false security through the same device, the unfulfillable prophecy. Ahab's tense and nervous speech is like Macbeth's, rather than Lear's. Both Macbeth and Ahab share a common hell of wicked, sleep-bursting dreams. They both endure the torture of isolation from humanity. The correspondence of these two evil worlds is precise. In either the divine has little place. Melville intended certain exclusions, and Christ and the Holy Ghost were two of them. Ahab, alas, could not even baptize in the name of the Father. He could only do it in the name of the Devil.

That is the Ahab-world, and it is wicked. Melville meant exactly what he wrote to Hawthorne when the book was consummated:

> I have written a wicked book, and feel as spotless as the lamb.

Melville's "wicked book" is the drama of Ahab, his hot hate for the White Whale, and his vengeful pursuit of it from the moment the ship plunges like fate into the Atlantic. It is that action, not the complete novel *Moby-Dick*. The *Moby-Dick* universe contains more, something different. Perhaps the difference is the reason why Melville felt "spotless as the lamb." The rough notes in the Shakespeare embrace it.

"Madness is undefinable." Two plays from which the thought could have sprung are in the volume in which it is written down: *Lear* and *Hamlet*. Of the modes of madness in *Lear*—the King's, the Fool's—which is definable? But we need not rest on supposition as to what Melville drew of madness from *Hamlet*, or from *Lear: Moby-Dick* includes both Ahab and Pip. Melville forces his analysis of Ahab's mania to incredible distances, only himself to admit that "Ahab's larger, darker, deeper part remains unhinted." Pip's is a more fathomable idiocy: "his shipmates called him mad." Melville challenges the description, refuses to leave Pip's madness dark and unhinted, declares: "So man's insanity is heaven's sense."

The emphasis in this declaration is the key to resolve apparent difficulties in the last sentence of the notes in the Shakespeare volume:

> It & right reason extremes of one,—not the (black art) Goetic but Theurgic magic—seeks converse with the Intelligence, Power, the Angel.

I take "it" to refer to the "madness" of the previous sentence. "Right reason," less familiar to the 20th century, meant more to the last, for in the Kant-Coleridge terminology "right reason" described the highest range of the intelligence and stood in contrast to "understanding." Melville had used the phrase in *Mardi*. What he did with it there discloses what meaning it had for him when he used it in these cryptic notes for the composition of *Moby-Dick*. *Mardi*:

> Right reason, and Alma (Christ), are the same; else Alma, not reason, would we reject. The Master's great command is Love; and here do all things wise, and all things good, unite. Love is all in all. The more we love, the more we know; and so reversed.

Now, returning to the notes, if the phrase "not the (black art) Goetic but Theurgic magic" is recognized as parenthetical, the sentence has some clarity: "madness" and its apparent opposite "right reason" are the two extremes of one way or attempt or urge to reach "the Intelligence, Power, the Angel" or, quite simply, God.

The adjectives of the parenthesis bear this reading out. "Goetic" might seem to derive from Goethe and thus *Faust*, but its source is the Greek "goetos," meaning variously trickster, juggler and, as here, magician. (Plato called literature "Goeteia") Wherever Melville picked up the word he means it, as he says, for the "black art." "Theurgic," in sharp contrast, is an accurate term for a kind of occult art of the Neoplatonists in which, through self-purification and sacred rites, the aid of the divine was evoked. In thus opposing "Goetic" and "Theurgic" Melville is using a distinction as old as Chaldea between black and white magic, the one of demons, the other of saints and angels, one evil, the other benevolent. For white or "Theurgic" magic, like "madness" and "right reason," seeks God, while the "black art Goetic" invokes only the devil.

Now go to *Moby-Dick*. In the Ahab-world there is no place for "converse with the Intelligence, Power, the Angel." Ahab cannot seek it, for understood between him and Fedallah is a compact as binding as Faust's with Mephistopheles. Melville's assumption is that though both Ahab and Faust may be seekers after truth, a league with evil closes the door to truth. Ahab's art, so long as his hate survives, is black. He does not seek true converse.

"Madness," on the contrary, does, and Pip is mad, possessed of an insanity which is "heaven's sense." When the little Negro almost drowned, his soul went down to wondrous depths and there he "saw God's foot upon the treadle of the loom, and spoke it." Through that accident Pip, of all the crew, becomes "prelusive of the eternal time" and thus achieves the converse Ahab has denied himself by his blasphemy. The chapter on THE DOUBLOON dramatizes the attempts on the part of the chief active characters to reach truth. In that place Starbuck, in his "mere unaided virtue," is revealed to have no abiding faith: he retreats before "Truth," fearing to lose his "righteousness." . . . Stubb's jollity and Flask's clod-like stupidity blunt the spiritual. . . . The Manxman has mere superstition, Queequeg mere curiosity. . . . Fedallah worships the doubloon evilly. . . . Ahab sees the gold coin solipsistically: "three peaks as proud as Lucifer" and all named "Ahab!"

Pip alone, of all, has true prescience: he names the doubloon the "navel" of the ship—"Truth" its life.

"Right reason" is the other way to God. It is the way of
man's sanity, the pure forging of his intelligence in the
smithy of life. To understand what use Melville made of
it in *Moby-Dick* two characters, both inactive to the plot,
have to be brought forth.

Bulkington is the man who corresponds to "right
reason." Melville describes him once early in the book
when he enters the Spouter Inn. "Six feet in height, with
noble shoulders, and a chest like a coffer-dam." In the
deep shadows of his eyes "floated some reminiscences that
did not seem to give him much joy." In the LEE SHORE
chapter Bulkington is explicitly excluded from the action
of the book, but not before Melville has, in ambiguities,
divulged his significance as symbol. Bulkington is Man
who, by "deep, earnest thinking" puts out to sea, scorning
the land, convinced that "in landlessness alone resides the
highest truth, shoreless, indefinite as God."

The rest of the *Pequod's* voyage Bulkington remains a
"sleeping-partner" to the action. He is the secret member
of the crew, below deck always, like the music under the
earth in *Antony and Cleopatra*, strange. He is the crew's
heart, the sign of their paternity, the human thing. And
by that human thing alone can they reach their apotheosis.

There remains Ishmael. Melville framed Ahab's action,
and the parts Pip, Bulkington and the rest of the crew
played in the action, within a narrative told by Ishmael.
Too long in criticism of the novel Ishmael has been con-
fused with Herman Melville himself. Ishmael is fictive,
imagined, as are Ahab, Pip and Bulkington, not so com-
pletely perhaps, for the very reason that he is so like his
creator. But he is not his creator only: he is a chorus
through whom Ahab's tragedy is seen, by whom what is
black and what is white magic is made clear. Like the

Catskill eagle Ishmael is able to dive down into the blackest gorges and soar out to the light again.

He is passive and detached, the observer, and thus his separate and dramatic existence is not so easily felt. But unless his choric function is recognized some of the vision of the book is lost. When he alone survived the wreck of the *Pequod*, he remained, after the shroud of the sea rolled on, to tell more than Ahab's wicked story. Ahab's self-created world, in essence privative, a thing of blasphemies and black magic, has its offset. Ahab has to dominate over a world where the humanities may also flower and man (the crew) by Pip's or Bulkington's way reach God. By this use of Ishmael Melville achieved a struggle and a catharsis which he intended, to feel "spotless as the lamb."

Ishmael has that cleansing ubiquity of the chorus in all drama, back to the Greeks. It is interesting that, in the same place where the notes for *Moby-Dick* are written in his Shakespeare, Melville jots down: "Eschylus Tragedies." Ishmael alone hears Father Mapple's sermon out. He alone saw Bulkington, and understood him. It was Ishmael who learned the secrets of Ahab's blasphemies from the prophet of the fog, Elijah. He recognized Pip's God-sight, and moaned for him. He cries forth the glory of the crew's humanity. Ishmael tells *their* story and *their* tragedy as well as Ahab's, and thus creates the *Moby-Dick* universe in which the Ahab-world is, by the necessity of life—or the Declaration of Independence—*included*.

Ahab and his fool

Life has its way, even with Ahab. Melville had drawn
upon another myth besides Shakespeare's to create his
dark Ahab, that of both Marlowe and Goethe: the Faust
legend. But he alters it. After the revolutions of the 18th-
19th century the archetype Faust has never been the same.
In Melville's alteration the workings of Lear and the Fool
can also be discerned.

The change comes in the relation of Ahab to Pip. Ahab
does not die in the tempestuous agony of Faustus pointing
to Christ's blood and crying for His mercy. He dies with
an acceptance of his damnation. Before his final battle
with the White Whale Ahab has resigned himself to his
fate.

His solipsism is most violent and his hate most engen-

dered the night of THE CANDLES when he raises the burning harpoon over his crew. It is a night of storm. The
setting is *Lear*-like. Ahab, unlike Lear, does not in this
night of storm discover his love for his fellow wretches.
On the contrary, this night Ahab uncovers his whole hate.
He commits the greater blasphemy than defiance of sun
and lightning. He turns the harpoon, forged and baptized
for the inhuman Whale alone, upon his own human com-
panions, the crew, and brandishes his hate over them. The
morning after the storm Ahab is most subtly dedicated
to his malignant purpose when he gives the lightning-
twisted binnacle a new needle. Melville marks this pitch
of his ego:

> In his fiery eyes of scorn and triumph, you then saw
> Ahab in all his fatal pride.

In a very few hours the change in Ahab sets in and Pip
—the shadow of Pip—is the agent of the change. Like a
reminder of Ahab's soul he calls to Ahab and Ahab, ad-
vancing to help, cries to the sailor who has seized Pip:
"Hands off that holiness!" It is a crucial act: for the first
time Ahab has offered to help another human being. And
at that very moment Ahab speaks Lear's phrases:

> Thou touchest my inmost centre, boy; thou art tied
> to me by cords woven of my heart-strings. Come, let's
> down.

Though Ahab continues to curse the gods for their "inhu-
manities," his tone, from this moment, is richer, quieter,
less angry and strident. He even questions his former
blasphemies, for a bottomed sadness grows in him as Pip
lives in the cabin with him. There occurs a return of
something Peleg had insisted that Ahab possessed on the
day Ishmael signed for the fatal voyage. Peleg then refuted
Ishmael's fears of his captain's wicked name—that dogs

had licked his blood. He revealed that Ahab had a wife and child, and concluded:

> hold ye then there can be any utter, hopeless harm in Ahab? No, no, my lad; stricken, blasted, if he be, Ahab has his humanities!

These humanities had been set aside in Ahab's hate for the White Whale. One incident: Ahab never thought, as he paced the deck at night in fever of anger, how his whalebone stump rapping the boards waked his crew and officers. The aroused Stubb confronts Ahab. Ahab orders him like a dog to kennel. For Stubb cannot, like Pip, affect Ahab. When it is over Stubb's only impulse is to go down on his knees and pray for the hot old man who he feels has so horribly amputated himself from human feelings.

Pip continues to be, mysteriously, the agent of this bloom once it has started. Says Ahab: "I do suck most wondrous philosophies from thee!" He even goes so far as to ask God to bless Pip and save him. BUT before he asks that, he threatens to murder Pip, Pip so weakens his revengeful purpose.

Though Pip recedes in the last chapters, the suppleness he has brought out of old Ahab continues to grow. Pip is left in the hold as though Ahab would down his soul once more, but above decks Ahab is no longer the proud Lucifer. He asks God to bless the captain of the *Rachel*, the last ship they meet before closing with Moby-Dick, the vessel which later picks Ishmael up after the tragedy. The difference in his speech is commented on: "a voice that prolongingly moulded every word." And it is noticed that when, toward the last days, Ahab prepares a basket lookout for himself to be hoisted up the mast to sight Moby-Dick, he trusts his "life-line" to Starbuck's hands. This running sap of his humanities gives out its last shoots in THE SYMPHONY chapter: observe that Ahab asks God to destroy what has been from the first his boast—"God! God! God! stave my brain!" He has turned to Starbuck and talked about his wife and child! And though this apple, his last, and cindered, drops to the soil, his revenge is now less pursued than resigned to. His thoughts are beyond the whale, upon easeful death.

In the three days' chase he is a tense, mastered, almost grim man. He sets himself outside humanity still, but he is no longer arrogant, only lonely: "Cold, cold . . ." After the close of the second day, when Fedallah cannot be found, he withers. His last vindictive shout is to rally his angers which have been hurled and lost like Fedallah and the harpoon of lightning and blood. He turns to Fate, the handspike in his windlass: "The whole act's immutably decreed." That night he does not face the whale as was his custom. He turns his "heliotrope glance" back to the east, waiting the sun of the fatal third day like death. It is Macbeth in his soliloquy of tomorrow, before Macduff will meet and match him. On the third day the unbodied winds engage his attention for the first time in the voyage. Even after the White Whale is sighted Ahab lingers, looks over the sea, considers his ship, says goodbye to his masthead. He admits to Starbuck he foreknows his death: the prophecies are fulfilled. In his last speech he moans only that his ship perishes without him:

> Oh, lonely death on lonely life! Oh, now I feel my topmost greatness lies in my topmost grief.

He rushes to the White Whale with his old curse dead on his lips.

The last words spoken to him from the ship had been Pip's: "O master, my master, come back!"

What Pip wrought in Ahab throws over the end of *Moby-Dick* a veil of grief, relaxes the tensions of its hate, and permits a sympathy for the stricken man that Ahab's insistent diabolism up to the storm would not have evoked. The end of this fire-forked tragedy is enriched by a pity in the very jaws of terror.

The lovely association of Ahab and Pip is like the relations of Lear to both the Fool and Edgar. What the King learns of their suffering through companionship with them in storm helps him to shed his pride. His hedging and self-deluding authority gone, Lear sees wisdom in their profound unreason. He becomes capable of learning from his Fool just as Captain Ahab does from his cabinboy.

In *Lear* Shakespeare has taken the conventional "crazy-witty" and brought him to an integral place in much more than the plot. He is at center to the poetic and dramatic conception of the play. Melville grasped the development.

Someone may object that Pip is mad, not foolish. In Shakespeare the gradations subtly work into one another. In *Moby-Dick* Pip is both the jester and the idiot. Before he is frightened out of his wits he and his tambourine are cap and bells to the crew. His soliloquy upon their midnight revelry has the sharp, bitter wisdom of the Elizabethan fool. And his talk after his "drowning" is parallel not only to the Fool and Edgar but to Lear himself.

A remark in *Moby-Dick* throws a sharp light over what has just been said and over what remains to be said. Melville comments on Pip:

> all thy strange mummeries not unmeaningly blended with the black tragedy of the melancholy ship, and mocked it.

For Pip by his madness had seen God.

Shakespeare, concluded

Melville was no naïve democrat. He recognized the persistence of the "great man" and faced, in 1850, what we have faced in the 20th century. At the time of the rise of the common man Melville wrote a tragedy out of the rise, and the fall, of uncommon Ahab.

In the old days of the Mediterranean and Europe it was the flaw of a king which brought tragedy to men. A calamity was that which "unwar strook the regnes that been proude." When fate was feudal, and a great man fell, his human property, the people, paid.

A whaleship reminded Melville of two things: (1) democracy had not rid itself of overlords; (2) the common man, however free, leans on a leader, the leader, however dedicated, leans on a straw. He pitched his tragedy right there.

America, 1850 was his GIVEN:

"a poor old whale-hunter" the great man;
fate, the chase of the Sperm whale, plot (economics
    is the administration of scarce resources);
the crew the commons, the Captain over them;

EQUALS:

tragedy.

For a consideration of dominance in man, read by all
means the chapter in *Moby-Dick* called THE SPECKSYNDER,
concerning emperors and kings, the forms and usages of
the sea:

through these forms that certain sultanism of Ahab's
brain became incarnate in an irresistible dictatorship.

For be a man's intellectual superiority what it will,
it can never assume the practical, available suprem-
acy over other men, without the aid of some sort of
external arts and entrenchments, always, in themselves, more or less paltry and base.

Nor will the tragic dramatist who would depict mortal indomitableness in its fullest sweep and direct
swing, ever forget a hint, incidentally so important
in his art, as the one now alluded to.

More, much more.
    Melville saw his creative problem clearly:

He had a prose world, a NEW.
But it was "tragedie," old.
Shakespeare gave him a bag of tricks.
        The Q.E.D.: *Moby-Dick*.

The shape of *Moby-Dick*, like the meaning of its action, has roots deep in THE PLAYS. Melville studied Shakespeare's craft. For example, *characterization*. In at least three places Melville analyzes *Hamlet*. There are two in *Pierre*. One enlarges upon the only note he writes in his copy of the play: "the great Montaignism of Hamlet." The third and most interesting passage is in *The Confidence Man*. There Melville makes a distinction between the making of "odd" and the creation of "original" characters in literature. Of the latter he allows only three: Milton's Satan, Quixote, and Hamlet. The original character is

> like a revolving Drummond light, raying away from itself all round it—everything is lit by it, everything starts up to it (mark how it is with Hamlet).

Melville likens the effect to "that which in Genesis attends upon the beginning of things." In the creation of Ahab Melville made the best use of that lesson he knew how.

Structure, likewise. *Moby-Dick* has a rise and fall like the movement of an Elizabethan tragedy. The first twenty-two chapters, in which Ishmael as chorus narrates the preparations for the voyage, are precedent to the action and prepare for it. Chapter XXIII is an interlude, THE LEE SHORE; Bulkington, because he is "right reason," is excluded from the tragedy. With the next chapter the book's drama begins. The first act ends in the QUARTER-DECK chapter, the first precipitation of action, which brings together for the first time Ahab, the crew, and the purpose of the voyage—the chase of the White Whale. All the descriptions of the characters, all the forebodings, all the hints are brought to their first manifestation.

Another interlude follows: Ishmael expands upon MOBY-DICK and THE WHITENESS OF THE WHALE.

Merely to summarize what follows, the book then moves

up to the meeting with the *Jeroboam* and her mad prophet Gabriel (chp. LXXI) and, after that, in a third swell, into the visit of Ahab to the *Samuel Enderby* to see her captain who had lost his arm as Ahab his leg to Moby-Dick (chp. C). The pitch of the action is the storm scene, THE CANDLES. From that point on Ahab comes to repose, fifth act, in his fate.

In this final movement Moby-Dick appears, for the first time. It is a mistake to think of the Whale as antagonist in the usual dramatic sense. (In democracy the antagonisms are wide.) The demonisms are dispersed, and Moby-Dick but the more assailable mass of them. In fact the actual physical whale finally present in *Moby-Dick* is more comparable to death's function in Elizabethan tragedy: when the white thing is encountered first, he is in no flurry, but quietly gliding through the sea, "a mighty mildness of repose in swiftness."

Obviously *Moby-Dick* is a novel and not a play. It contains creations impossible to any stage—a ship the *Pequod*, whales, Leviathan, the vast sea. In the making of most of his books Melville used similar things. In *Moby-Dick* he integrated them as he never had before nor was to again.

The whaling matter is stowed away as he did not manage the ethnology of *Typee* nor was to, the parables of *The Confidence Man*. While the book is getting under way—that is, in the first forty-eight chapters—Melville allows only four "scientific" chapters on whaling to appear. Likewise as the book sweeps to its tragic close in the last thirty chapters, Melville rules out all such exposition. The body of the book supports the bulk of the matter on the Sperm whale—"scientific or poetic." Melville carefully controls these chapters, skillfully breaking them up: the eight different vessels the *Pequod* meets as she moves across the oceans slip in and cut between the considerations of cetology. Actually and deliberately the whaling chapters brake the advance of the plot. Van Wyck Brooks called them "ballast."

Stage directions appear throughout. *Soliloquies,* too. There is a significant use of the special Elizabethan soliloquy to the skull in Ahab's mutterings to the Sperm whale's head in THE SPHINX (chp. LXX). One of the subtlest *supernatural effects,* the "low laugh from the hold" in the QUARTER-DECK scene, echoes Shakespeare's use of the Ghost below ground in *Hamlet.*

Properties are used for precise theater effect. Ahab smashes his quadrant as Richard his mirror. Of them the Doubloon is the most important. Once Ahab has nailed the coin to the mast it becomes FOCUS. The imagery, the thought, the characters, the events precedent and to come, are centered on it. It is there, midstage, Volpone, gold.

Of the soliloquies Ahab's show the presence of *Elizabethan speech* most. The cadences and acclivities of Melville's prose change. Melville characterized Ahab's language as "nervous, lofty." In the soliloquies it is jagged like that of a Shakespeare hero whose speech like his heart often cracks in the agony of fourth and fifth act.

The long ease and sea swell of Ishmael's narrative prose contrasts this short, rent language of Ahab. The opposition of cadence is part of the counterpoint of the book. It adumbrates the part the two characters play, Ishmael the passive, Ahab the active. More than that, it arises from and returns, contrapunto, to the whole concept of the book revealed by the notes in Melville's copy of Shakespeare—the choric Ishmael can, like the Catskill eagle, find the light, but Ahab, whose only magic is Goetic, remains dark. The contrast in prose repeats the theme of calm and tempest which runs through the novel. Without exception action rises out of calm, whether it is the first chase of a whale, the appearance of the Spirit Spout, the

storm, or the final chase of Moby-Dick precipitously following upon THE SYMPHONY.

As the strongest literary force Shakespeare caused Melville to approach tragedy in terms of the drama. As the
strongest social force America caused him to approach
tragedy in terms of democracy.

It was not difficult for Melville to reconcile the two.
Because of his perception of America: Ahab.

It has to do with size, and how you value it. You can
approach BIG America and spread yourself like a pan-
cake, sing her stretch as Whitman did, be puffed up as
we are over PRODUCTION. It's easy. THE AMERI-
CAN WAY. Soft. Turns out paper cups, lies flat on the
brush. N.G.

Or recognize that our power is simply QUANTITY.
Without considering purpose. Easy too. That is, so long
as we continue to be INGENIOUS about machines, and
have the resources.

Or you can take an attitude, the creative vantage. See
her as OBJECT in MOTION, something to be shaped,
for use. It involves a first act of physics. You can observe
POTENTIAL and VELOCITY separately, have to, to
measure THE THING. You get approximate results.
They are usable enough if you include the Uncertainty
Principle, Heisenberg's law that you learn the speed at
the cost of exact knowledge of the energy and the energy
at the loss of exact knowledge of the speed.

Melville did his job. He calculated, and cast Ahab.
BIG, first of all. ENERGY, next. PURPOSE: lordship
over nature. SPEED: of the brain. DIRECTION: vengeance. COST: the people, the Crew.

Ahab is the FACT, the Crew the IDEA. The Crew is
where what America stands for got into *Moby-Dick*.
They're what we imagine democracy to be. They're Melville's addition to tragedy as he took it from Shakespeare.

He had to do more with the people than offstage shouts
in a *Julius Caesar*. This was the difference a Declaration
of Independence made. In his copy of the play Melville
writes the note

TAMMANY HALL

in heavy strokes beside Casca's description of the Roman
rabble before Caesar:

> If the tag-rag people did not clap him and hiss him,
> according as he pleas'd and displeas'd them, as they
> use to do the players in the theatre, I am no true
> man.

Melville thought he had more searoom to tell the truth.
He was writing in a country where an Andrew Jackson
could, as he put it, be "hurled higher than a throne."
A political system called "democracy" had led men to
think they were "free" of aristocracy. The fact of the
matter is Melville couldn't help but give the "people" a
larger part because in the life around him they played a
larger part. He put it this way:

> this august dignity I treat of, is not the dignity of
> kings and robes, but that abounding dignity which
> has no robed investiture.

> Thou shalt see it shining in the arm that wields a
> pick and drives a spike; that democratic dignity
> which, on all hands, radiates without end from God;
> Himself! The great God absolute! The center and
> circumference of all democracy! His omnipresence,
> our divine equality!

> If, then, to meanest mariners, and renegades and
> castaways, I shall hereafter ascribe high qualities,
> though dark; weave round them tragic graces; if
> even the most mournful, perchance the most abased,

among them all, shall at times lift himself to the exalted mounts; if I shall touch that workman's arm with some ethereal light; if I shall spread a rainbow over his disastrous set of sun; then against all mortal critics bear me out in it, thou just Spirit of Equality, which hast spread one royal mantle of humanity over all my kind!

Remember Bulkington.

To MAGNIFY is the mark of *Moby-Dick*. As with workers, castaways, so with the scope and space of the sea, the prose, the Whale, the Ship and, OVER ALL, the Captain. It is the technical act compelled by the American fact. Cubits of tragic stature. Put it this way. Three forces operated to bring about the dimensions of *Moby-Dick*: Melville, a man of MYTH, antemosaic; an experience of SPACE, its power and price, America; and ancient magnitudes of TRAGEDY, Shakespeare.

It is necessary now to consider *Antony and Cleopatra*, the play Melville pencilled most heavily. Rome was the World, and Shakespeare gives his people and the action imperial size. His hero and heroine love as Venus and Mars, as planets might.

> His legs bestrid the ocean; his rear'd arm
> Crested the world.

So Cleopatra dreamed of Antony. Melville marked her words. He marked Antony's joyful greeting to Cleopatra after he has beaten Caesar back to his camp:

> O thou day o' th' world!

And Cleopatra's cry of grief when Antony dies:

The crown o' th' earth doth melt.

Antony and Cleopatra is an East. It is built as Pyramids
were built. There is space here, and objects big enough
to contest space. These are men and women who live life
large. The problems are the same but they work themselves out on a stage as wide as ocean.

When Enobarbus comments on Antony's flight from
Actium in pursuit of Cleopatra, we are precisely within
the problems of *Moby-Dick*:

> To be furious
> Is to be frighted out of fear, and in that mood
> The dove will peck the estridge. I see still
> A diminution in our captain's brain
> Restores his heart. When valour preys on reason
> It eats the sword it fights with.

In exactly what way Ahab, furious and without fear, re-
tained the instrument of his reason as a lance to fight the
White Whale is a central concern of Melville's in *Moby-
Dick*. In his Captain there was a diminution in his heart.

From whaling, which America had made distinctly a
part of her industrial empire, he took this "poor old
whale-hunter," as he called him, this man of "Nantucket
grimness and shagginess." Out of such stuff he had to
make his tragic hero, his original. He faced his difficulties.
He knew he was denied "the outward majestical trappings
and housings" that Shakespeare had for his Antony, his
Lear and his Macbeth. Melville wrote:

> Oh, Ahab! what shall be grand in thee, must needs
> be plucked at from the skies, and dived for in the
> deep, and featured in the unbodied air!

He made him "a khan of the plank, and a king of the

sea, and a great lord of leviathans." For the American has the Roman feeling about the world. It is his, to dispose of. He strides it, with possession of it. His property. Has he not conquered it with his machines? He bends its resources to his will. The pax of legions? the Americanization of the world. Who else is lord?

Melville isolates Ahab in "a Grand-Lama-like exclusiveness." He is captain of the *Pequod* because of "that certain sultanism of his brain." He is proud and morbid, willful, vengeful. He wears a "hollow crown," not Richard's. It is the Iron Crown of Lombardy which Napoleon wore. Its jagged edge, formed from a nail of the Crucifixion, galls him. He worships fire and swears to strike the sun.

OVER ALL, hate—huge and fixed upon the imperceptible. Not man but all the hidden forces that terrorize man is assailed by the American Timon. That HATE, extra-human, involves his Crew, and Moby-Dick drags them to their death as well as Ahab to his, a collapse of a hero through solipsism which brings down a world.

At the end of the book, in the heart of the White Whale's destruction, the Crew and Pip and Bulkington and Ahab lie down together.

All scatt'red in the bottom of the sea.

FACT # 2 **dromenon**

FACT # 2

On the night of January 26, 1824, as the Nantucket whaleship the *Globe* cruised in the Pacific Ocean off Fannings Island, latitude 3 49′ North, longitude 158 29′ West, one of the vessel's two harpooneers, called boat-steerers, Samuel B. Comstock, aged 21, the son of a Quaker schoolmaster of Nantucket and a descendent on his mother's side of the Mitchells, a family as organic to the life of the island as the Coffins, Starbucks, Gardners and Macys, went down into the cabin shortly after 12 o'clock and, with a short axe, split the Captain's head in two as he slept, killed the Chief Mate the same way, confronted the two remaining officers with the cry, "I am the bloody man, I have the bloody hand and I will have revenge," shot the Third Mate with a musket and left the Second Mate dying from the wounds he gave him with a boarding knife, a two-edge instrument four feet long, three inches wide, used in whaling to cut the blubber from the body of a whale.

PART THREE

Moses

The book of the law of the blood

In *Moby-Dick* the sea, its creature, and man are all savage. The Whale is "athirst for human blood." Ahab has "that that's bloody on his mind." The sea will "forever and forever, to the crack of doom, insult and murder man."

It is cannibalism. Even Ishmael, the orphan who survives the destruction, cries out: "I myself am a savage, owing no allegiance but to the King of Cannibals; and ready at any moment to rebel against him."

It is the facts, to a first people.

(Nothing is without efficient cause)

1   Melville wanted a god. Space was the First, before time, earth, man. Melville sought it: "Polar eternities" behind "Saturn's gray chaos." Christ, a Holy Ghost, Jehovah never satisfied him. When he knew peace it was with a god of Prime. His dream was Daniel's: the Ancient of Days, garment white as snow, hair like the pure wool. Space was the paradise Melville was exile of.

When he made his whale he made his god. Ishmael once comes on the bones of a Sperm whale pitched up on land. They are massive, and he is struck with horror at the "antemosaic unsourced existence of the unspeakable terrors of the whale."

When Moby-Dick is first seen he swims a snow-hill on the sea. To Ishmael he is the white bull Jupiter swimming to Crete with ravished Europa on his horns: a prime, lovely, malignant, white.

2   Melville was agonized over paternity. He suffered as a son. He had lost the source. He demanded to know the father.

Kronos, in order to become god, armed himself with a sickle and castrated his father Uranus. Saturn used a pruning knife. Kronos and Saturn in turn were overthrown by their sons banded together in a brother horde. The new gods of Jupiter were, in their turn, attacked by other sons. These sons—they were the "Giants"—lost. They are described as more akin to men.

Enceladus was among them. He is a constant image in Melville. Melville saw his likeness in defeated and exiled heroes, not in successful sons who, by their triumph, become the fathers.

3   The fable of *Moby-Dick* is vengeance. On a previous voyage Ahab and the White Whale had met and fought. The whale had suddenly swept "his sickle-shaped

lower jaw beneath him" and reaped away Ahab's leg—"as a mower a blade of grass in the field."

(Osiris, Egyptian hero and god, was mangled by his son and enemy Seth in the shape of a boar, rent into fourteen pieces and scattered on the Nile, where fish ate his phallus.)

Ahab then had one purpose: "an audacious, immitigable, and supernatural revenge." For Ahab "piled upon the whale's white hump the sum of all the general rage and hate felt by his whole race from Adam down."

4   It is necessary to understand this rage and hate. Melville is not Jonathan Edwards. His answer to the angry god is an Ahab, a man of elements not of sins:

> Talk not to me of blasphemy, man; I'd strike the sun if it insulted me.

Melville's ethic is mythic. Shame with him was precedent to any Eden, was of Prime: the concord of Space, "sweet milk" to Melville as universal peace was to Shakespeare's Malcolm, was curdled and made sour by man, and blood.

It was not acts but Act, Original Act, that gave man guilt. Man's "imperial theme" is the fruit of First Murder.

Crime is large and imponderable when a man's experience of violence is mutiny, on wide sea. To kill a Captain!

Conscience is not the caliper to measure it:

> (remember the story of the ship the *Town-Ho* in *Moby-Dick?* who can pass judgment on Steelkilt when it is the White Whale who executes justice on the First Mate, Radney?)

immediately that Macbeth murders the King he strides hugely forward into the mystery. He steps from Scotland into the spheres to be damned:

> Thou seest the heavens, as troubled with man's act
> Threaten his bloody stage.

Space and time were not abstraction but the body of Melville's experience, and he cast the struggle in their dimension. The White Whale became the biggest single creature a man has been pitted against and Ahab's rage and hate is scaled like Satan's, the largest enemy of the Father man has imagined.

5   Ahab's birth was dark, uncanonical. Starbuck took him for "more demon than man." To Stubb he was "old man of oceans." Ishmael saw him "gnawed within and scorched without." Ahab felt himself to be "deadly faint, bowed and humped as though I were Adam."

Ahab had known an earlier terror than the sea. He had woe on him. He was branded with a "slender rod-like mark, lividly whitish" the length of him. The prophet Elijah told Ishmael that Ahab lay in a trance like dead for three days and nights off Cape Horn. At another time he looked like a man cut away from a stake.

The night of THE CANDLES, when lightning turns his masts to tapers, Ahab seizes the conductor chains of his ship. He does it, he says, to match his blood with fire. He cries up into the night:

> Oh, thou clear spirit, of thy fire thou madest me, and like a true child of fire, I breathe it back to thee.

(There is a myth that Prometheus did more than steal fire from the sun and bring it down to man: it is said that Prometheus fathered man.)

6   In *Moby-Dick*, when Ishmael has said all he can say about Ahab, he admits that the larger, darker, deeper part of the man is obscure. He suggests the same holds true for any man and insists it is necessary to go down to

a place far beneath a man's upper earth in order to un-
cover the unknown part.

There, he says, a man will find that his root of grandeur,
his whole awful essence sits in bearded state

>   an antique buried beneath antiquities and throned
>   on torsos.

Ishmael makes this comment:

>   So, with a broken throne, the great gods mock that
>   captive king.

He answers his own question who the king is:

>   it is your own grim sire, who did beget ye, exiled
>   sons.

Then, for a climax, offers this enigma:

>   from him only will the old State-secret come.

The Melville who wrote *Moby-Dick* had a firm hold on
that secret. He was a strong and sure-footed son as a result. He was not weakened by any new testament world.
He had reached back to where he belonged. He could
face up to Moses: he knew the great deed and misdeed of
primitive time. It was in himself.

This once he had his answer—how man acquires the
lost dimension of space. There is a way to disclose paternity, declare yourself the rival of earth, air, fire and
water.

Now he counted his birthdays as the Hebrews did: a
son's years gathered not from the son's birth but from the
father's death. Another Moses Melville wrote in *Moby-
Dick* the Book of the Law of the Blood.

PART FOUR

Christ

for

EDWARD DAHLBERG, my other genius of the Cross and the Windmills. If the Fool is in this book, you nurtured him.

Melville read *Don Quixote* as you have. He did it at a most important time, when he was turning for succor, as I imagine you have turned, to the Mediterranean world, and Christ. He acquired his copy in September, 1855.

Two of the passages he marked belong to your experience as to his. I want you particularly to have them:

> Sancho Panza alone believed all that his master said to be true, knowing who he was, and having been acquainted with him from his birth.

The other is Don Antonio's cry against all the Simon Carrascos of life who gloat when they have unseated a poor Knight:

> Oh! sir, God forgive you the injury you have done the whole world, in endeavoring to restore to his senses the most diverting madman in it.

Christ

In 1841 Melville had gone to the Pacific. In 1856 he went to the Holyland. It is in such contrast that the work of his last forty years, from *Moby-Dick* in 1851 to his death in New York in 1891, stands to the Pacific experience and the books which issued from it: *Typee, Omoo, Mardi, White-Jacket,* and *Moby-Dick.*

The trip of 1856 is an unnatural twin to the better known earlier voyage. He made it at a critical time in his career and it tells, as story, what is the truth, as I see it, of his loss of power.*

* The principal acts of the last forty years are:

Pierre, a novel of New York, written 1851-2 (1852);

"Bartleby the Scrivener," "The Encantadas" and "Benito Cereno," three important short prose pieces, two of them throw-backs to the Pacific; first

When he set out in October of that year he had reasons of health for doing so. The writing of *Moby-Dick* had hurt him. He was 31. The immediate labor on *Pierre* aggravated his condition. It went so far his family in 1853 called in doctors, among them Oliver Wendell Holmes, Pittsfield neighbor, to judge his sanity.

As early as 1851 Melville had figured it would help if he got away. A relative who came to call in December shortly after the publication of *Moby-Dick* reported her conversation with Melville to Duyckinck in New York:

> I laughed at him somewhat and told him that the recluse life he was leading made his city friends think that he was slightly insane—he replied that long ago he came to the same conclusion himself but if he left home to look after Hungary the cause in hunger would suffer.

By 1856 and the writing of *The Confidence-Man*, wild and whirling words, the whole persistent multitude of Melvilles and Shaws felt that something had to be done, that there had to be some disposition, once and for all, of this man whom some tolerated and others feared, and of whom most were ashamed and all seemed weary. The money for the trip came from his father-in-law, Justice Shaw. This time Melville did not go away on his own; he was—though guardedly—sent away.

---

published in Putnam's Monthly Magazine, 1853, '54, '55, collected in *The Piazza Tales* (1856);

The Confidence-Man, a novel called a "masquerade," apparently written from 1854 to 1856 (1857);

the Holyland journey, October 1856-May 1857;

verse from 1859 on, including the two-volume narrative in four parts *Clarel, A Poem and Pilgrimage in the Holyland* (1876);

and the return to prose, *Billy Budd, Foretopman*, a short novel, written 1888-91, found in mss. 1919.

In England, to book passage on a Mediterranean steamer, he visited Hawthorne. Hawthorne describes him as "looking much as he used to do (a little paler, and perhaps a little sadder), a rough outside coat, and with his characteristic gravity and reserve of manner." The two men spent a day by the sea near Southport, sheltering themselves from the wind in a hollow among the sandhills. They had what Melville calls in his journal simply "good talk." Hawthorne, in his, says more:

> Melville, as he always does, began to reason of Providence and futurity, and of everything that lies beyond human ken, and informed me that he had 'pretty much made up his mind to be annihilated'; but still he does not seem to rest in that anticipation, and, I think, will never rest until he gets hold of a definite belief.

> It is strange how he persists—and has persisted ever since I knew him, and probably long before—in wandering to and fro over these deserts, as dismal and monotonous as the sandhills amid which we were sitting. He can neither believe, nor be comfortable in his unbelief; and he is too honest and courageous not to try to do one or the other.

> If he were a religious man, he would be one of the most truly religious and reverential; he has a very high and noble nature and is better worth immortality than most of us.

Hawthorne saw Melville again the day before he sailed: "He said that he already felt better than in America; but observed that he did not anticipate much pleasure in his rambles, for the spirit of adventure is gone out of him. He certainly is much overshadowed since I saw him last; but I hope he will brighten as he goes onward."

Seven years earlier, before *Moby-Dick*, Melville had almost made the same trip. 1849, at sea, bound for England to sell *White-Jacket*:

> This afternoon Dr Taylor and I sketched a plan for going down the Danube from Vienna to Constantinople; thence to Athens on the steamer; to Beyroot and Jerusalem—Alexandria and the Pyramids . . .

> I am full (just now) of this glorious Eastern jaunt. Think of it: Jerusalem and the Pyramids!—Constantinople, the Aegean and also Athens!

Age 37 now, Melville goes to the Mediterranean world to refresh himself. He offers himself, as he says, a "passive subject" to a more immediate past than at 21 he had found in primitive Polynesia.

He does not bring back a *Typee*. The *Journal Up the Straits* is an uncreated thing. It is the record of Melville's rediscovery of the East and then, his loss of it. The story can be told now that Raymond Weaver has, after much labor, made the text available. It lies under the *Journal's* illegible surface.

The sun and the darker races stirred up feelings Melville had for twelve years beaten back, even as he worked. In spite of his writing he had become wedded to a white guilt. The pressures had originated from his environment America and tightened inwards. The stifling forces had a traitorous agent to help them: the ethical and Northern Melville.

There seems no doubt he brought back from the South Seas a number of shames, social shames to add to earlier ones reaching back to his father's sins and failures. Melville's behavior in the years 1851-56 was ill. He remained periodically violent to his wife, and strange with his mother. There was shock in him. *Pierre* is documentation enough. Add *The Confidence-Man*. In each Christ is of the subject and the matter.

In the *Journal Up the Straits* the story of Melville's return starts after Cape Finisterre is passed, off Cape Vincent. The entry for that day is a dumb show of what is to follow. The contraries of the man who now turns to the East for some resolution of them lie in these natural sentences, as outward as gestures:

Sunday, Nov. 23, 1856

Sunday 23d. Passed within a third of a mile of Cape St. Vincent. Light house & monastery on bold cliff. Cross. Cave underneath light house. The whole Atlantic breaks here. Lovely afternoon. Great procession of ships bound for Crimea must have been descried from this point.

Melville had started a ghost. What he sees on the cliff is, quick, his, life: HEIGHT and CAVE, with the CROSS between. And his books are made up of these things: light house, monastery, Cross, cave, the Atlantic, an afternoon, the Crimea: truth, celibacy, Christ, the great dark, space of ocean, the senses, man's past.

First act, the Mediterranean. It is reiteration, it might have been rite. Melville makes this entry his first day on it: "Pacific." A Noah, Melville had dominated and survived his Flood. *Moby-Dick*, ark, is behind him, and so are the waters of his Flood, the Atlantic and the Pacific. He returns to smaller waters, the Mediterranean. "In landlessness alone resides the highest truth, shoreless, indefinite as God," Melville had written, to characterize Bulkington, in the LEE SHORE chapter of *Moby-Dick*.

The Mediterranean is a close sea, is in the middle of the land, is the old center of earth. On its shores Noah's chil-

dren, Shem, Ham and Japeth, and their sons, have worked
out life since flood. Melville had the alternative Noah had
when the waters shrank: to be a husbandman. There was
much for him to do—as much had been done—from
Genesis on, before Christ. Melville had room in an old
testament world, ample space and time to reify. There
was a Covenant for him to share, the everlasting one between God and every living creature of all flesh that is
upon the earth. The pity of it, in 1856, is this: the only
place Melville manages to see the token of covenant, the
rainbow, is over the waters of the Dead Sea.

He missed his own truth. The Atlantic, the Pacific and
the Mediterranean formed a trinity more natural to him,
as poète d'espace, than that other Trinity, that desert he
chose to wander to and fro in, his last forty years. "Ego
non baptizo te in nomine Patris et Filii et Spiritus Sancti
—sed in nomine Diaboli."

Constantinople gave Melville back to sensation. He had
shown a marked interest in the women of two harems
aboard ship on the passage in. He likens the city to a
woman: "The fog lifted from about the skirts of the
city . . . It was a coy disclosure, a kind of coquetting . . .
like her Sultanas she was thus seen veiled in her 'ash-
mack.' " It is an unusual image for Melville to use. There
is not only an absence of palpable woman in his works,
there is rarely a sense of what accompanies her, clothes,
charm, pleasure. Fayaway, of *Typee*, perhaps, as a memory, a dream. There are the two pairs, Lucy and Isabel of
Pierre and their prototypes, Yillah and Hautia of *Mardi*.
And there is only one other, the best of them, the Chola
Widow of "The Encantadas," who takes body from the tale
of her suffering.

The two pairs are unfelt and unfleshed. Hautia is a
Pacific island "Queen" whom Melville, in trying to turn
into a Salem witch, handles as gingerly as Cotton Mather

did poor Margaret Rule. She is unburnt, unconfessed, her "zone unbound," "brazen" and inviting, "I the vortex that draws all in," absurd. Isabel too. She is Melville's chromo Cenci, sorceress and "sister" to Pierre, their common spell a lampish incest. Lucy, meant to be as Yillah a contrast, is a "betrothed" who sketches and sews, a chalkish lady, a lace of "earthly frailty" who can give Pierre nothing but a text: "heaven hath called me to a wonderful office toward thee"!

That Melville did, on this trip, at Constantinople and elsewhere, find some spontaneity toward woman suggests a change in the contours of his psyche profound enough to free forces in him long checked. He ranges the polyglot city wildly, writes about it extravagantly. He mixes in the crowds of the suburbs of Galata and Pera. He mounts the bridges to watch them moving below. When he leans over the First Bridge his body is alive as it has not been since he swung with Jack Chase in maintops above the Pacific. The difference: he is brooding over a city of a million and a half human beings, not so many square miles of empty ocean:

> To the Bazaar. A wilderness of traffic. Furniture, arms, silks, confectionery, shoes, sandles—everything. (Cairo). Crowded overhead with stone arches, with side openings.

> Immense crowds. Georgians, Armenians, Greeks, Jews, & Turks are the merchants. Magnificent embroidered silks & gilt sabres & caparisons for horses.

> You loose yourself & are bewildered & confounded with the labyrinth, the din, the barbaric confusion of the whole.

> The Propontis, the Bosphorus, the Golden Horn, the domes, the minarets, the bridges, the men of war, the cypresses. Indescribable.

What is common to all passages is the attention to the human and natural, the concrete, what has been husbanded. Architecture buds and leafs. He finds the source of the mosque dome in the tents of the nomadic tribes, the form of the minaret in the cypress tree. Asia and Europe confronting each other at the Bosphorus are two women in "a contest of beauty." The color of Asia is "like those Asiatic lions one sees in menageries—lazy & torpid."

   Turn your attention now to stone. To stone as it is. As it is built with. As it is rubble.

   Turn first to standing stone, to Egypt. The *Journal* comes to climax before the Pyramids.

   Whether it is the appropriation of space involved or the implied defiance of time or the enceladic assault on the heavens, MASONRY is especially associated with MYTH in man. The tale of the Great Tower is as ultimate a legend as the Flood, Eden, Adam.

   Whatever the explanation of the great pyramid at Cholula or the source of Plato's description of the watchtowers of Atlantis, they, like the Pyramids, partake of this need of man to persist in monument as well as in myth. The temple of the sun at Babel was named E-sagila, meaning, the House of the Lifting of the Head.

   THE PYRAMIDS loom, a long slope of crags and precipices; the tablerock overhanging, adhering solely by mortar, twisted at angles like broken cliffs. Masonry—and is it man's? The lines of stone do not seem like courses of masonry, but like strata of rocks. Slanting up the sweeping flanks people move like mules on the Andes. They ascend guided by Arabs in flowing white mantles, conducted as by angels. These are the steps Jacob lay at.

   I shudder at the idea of the ancient Egyptians. It

was in these pyramids that the idea of Jehovah was born. A terrible mixture of the cunning and the awful. Moses was learned in all the lore of the Egyptians.

No wall, no roof. In other buildings, however vast, the eye is gradually innured to the sense of magnitude, by passing from part to part. But here there is no stay or stage. It is all or nothing. It is not the sense of height or breadth or length or depth that is stirred. It is the sense of immensity that is stirred.

The theory that they were built as a defense against the desert is absurd. They might have been created with the Creation.

As with the ocean, you learn as much of its vastness by the first five minutes' glance as you would in a month, so with the pyramid.

Its simplicity confounds you. Finding it vain to take in the sea's vastness man has taken to sounding it and weighing its density; so with the pyramid, he measures the base and computes the size of individual stones. It refuses to be studied or adequately comprehended. It still looms in my imagination, dim and indefinite.

The tearing away of the casing, though it removed enough stone to build a walled-town, has not one whit subtracted from the apparent magnitude. It has had just the contrary effect. When the pyramid presented a smooth plane, it must have lost as much in impressiveness as the ocean does when unfurrowed. A dead calm of masonry. But now the ridges majestically diversify.

It has been said in panegyric of some extraordinary works of man, that they affect the imagination like the works of Nature. But the pyramid affects one in neither way exactly. Man seems to have had as little to do with it as Nature.

It was that supernatural creature, the priest. They must needs have been terrible inventors, those Egyptian wise men. And one seems to see that, as out of the crude forms of the natural earth they could evoke by art the transcendent mass and symmetry and awe of the pyramid, so out of the rude elements of the insignificant thoughts that are in all men, they could rear the transcendent conception of a God.

But for no holy purpose was the pyramid founded.

Nor *Moby-Dick* written. But see how Melville turned, turned to stone as it is rubble, to Judea:

Stones of Judea. We read a good deal about stones in Scriptures. Monuments & memorials are set up of stones; men are stoned to death; the figurative seed falls in stony places; and no wonder . . . Judea is one accumulation of stones.

It is LAST ACT. When Melville went from the Pyramids to Jerusalem he lost all he had gained. The power so to describe the Pyramids leaves him, as did the power to do *Moby-Dick*, prey to Christ. He had observed in Egypt that the Sphinx has its "back to desert & face to verdure." Melville reversed his Sphinx. He thought he faced verdure in Christ. It turned out to be desert.

Barrenness of Judea

Whitish mildew pervading whole tracts of landscape —bleached—leprosy—encrustation of curses . . . bones of rocks, —crunched, knawed, & mumbled—mere refuse & rubbish of creation . . .

No moss as in other ruins—no grace of decay—no ivy —the unleavened nakedness of desolation—whitish ashes—lime-kilns—You see the anatomy—compares with ordinary regions as skeleton with living & rosy man.

Two weeks in the Holyland sealed Melville in a bitterness of disillusion from which he never recovered, out of which, fifteen years later, he wrote *Clarel*, that rosary of doubt, a two-volume *Poem and Pilgrimage in the Holyland* and, thirty-odd years later, *Billy Budd*, that most Christian tale of a ship, and mutiny. The stones, the rubble in the pool of Bethseda, Sodom's "bitumen & ashes," the Dead Sea with the foam on its beach "like slaver of mad dog," and the Holy Sepulcher "a sickening cheat" led Melville to one final question:

> Is the desolation of the land the result of the fatal embrace of the Deity?

Melville became Christ's victim, and it was death, and· lack of love, that let him be it. "Poor soul, the centre of my sinful earth," Shakespeare wrote. Melville became unsure of the center. It had been strong, a backward and downward in him like Ahab's, like a pyramid's:

> The old mummy lies buried in cloth on cloth; it takes time to unwrap this Egyptian king.

With the coming of despair he called it a bulb of nothing. In the middle of the writing of *Moby-Dick* he wrote to Hawthorne:

> But I feel that I am now come to the inmost leaf of the bulb, and that shortly the flower must fall to the mould.

In *Pierre*—it was between these two books that the change came—he wrote:

> By vast pains we mine into the pyramid; by horrible gropings we come to the central room; with joy we espy the sarcophagus; but we lift the lid—and no body is there! —appallingly vacant as vast is the soul of man!

He denied himself in Christianity. It is space, and its feeding on man, that is the essence of his vision, bred in him here in America, and it is time which is at the heart of Christianity. What the Pacific had confirmed for him he allowed Christ to undo. It was on the promise of a future life that Melville caught.

Death bothered him. That bare-headed life under the grass, his own, worried him, in Dickinson's words, like a wasp. He looked for solace to the Resurrection. He got nothing. For the loss of mortality he got nothing in return. The dimensions of life as he had felt them merely dwindled. Objects lost their gravity as they bulk in space.

All he has left in 1856 is the shell of his own faith: he tells Hawthorne he has "pretty much made up his mind to be annihilated." The charge Melville levels at Christ in *Clarel* is the lie in the promise of life beyond death:

> Behold him—yea—behold the Man
> Who warranted if not began
> The dream that drags out its repulse.

He mocks Christ with His own cry to the Father, why hast Thou forsaken me:

> Upbraider! we upbraid again.

The sense of life and death that Melville forfeited is one the experience of space gives. The vision of it is *Moby-Dick*, and its savage myth. In *Pierre* it is reduced, as Melville was, to statement. There are two passages which speak out, fatty as the prose is. They may say why

Christ hampered him. One is a celebration of Enceladus
for his war with the other Giants to reclaim his birthright
from the father. That was battle for mortality as Melville
understood it best, and on which his imagination fed.
The other passage celebrates annihilation freed from the
doubt Christ brought:

> Of old Greek times, before man's brain went into
> doting bondage, and bleached and beaten in Bacon-
> ian fulling-mills, his four limbs lost their barbaric
> tan and beauty; when the round world was fresh,
> and rosy, and spicy, as a new-plucked apple; —all's
> wilted now!—in those bold times, the great dead
> were not, turkey-like, dished in trenchers, and set
> down all garnished in the ground, to glut the damned
> Cyclop like a cannibal; but nobly envious life cheated
> the glutton worm, and gloriously burned the corpse;
> so that the spirit up-pointed, and visibly forked to
> heaven!

Somewhere Yeats uses the phrase "sighing after Jerusalem in the regions of the grave." Christ's slide of future
life deflected Melville's sight of past. Melville had made
his act of faith in *Mardi*: "My memory is a life beyond
birth." His natural sense of time was in its relation to
space. It was not diverted as Christ's was, away from object, to the individual, and the passage of the personal
soul. To Melville the intimate and the concrete of the
present, as for example he felt it at Constantinople, enabled a man to loose himself into space and time and, in
their dimensions, to feel and comprehend such an object
as the Pyramids, to create, in like dimensions, an Ahab
and a White Whale. Time was not a line drawn straight
ahead toward future, a logic of good and evil. Time returned on itself. It had density, as space had, and events
were objects accumulated within it, around which men

could move as they moved in space. The acts of men as a group stood, put down in time, as a pyramid was, to be reexamined, reenacted. He wrote in *Mardi*:

> Do you believe that you lived three thousand years ago? No. But for me, I was at the subsiding of the Deluge, and helped swab the ground, and build the first house.

> With the Israelites, I fainted in the wilderness; was in court when Solomon outdid all the judges before him.

> I, it was, who suppressed the lost work of Manteo, on the Egyptian theology, as containing mysteries not to be revealed to posterity, and things at war with the canonical scriptures.

Melville was.

I have called *Moby-Dick* a book of the Old Dispensation. Christ's dispensation was as strange to Melville as it would have been to the First Adam.

Hawthorne was right, Melville could not rest without a belief, he had to have a god. In *Moby-Dick* he had one. I called him the Ancient of Days. The job was a giant's, to make a new god. To do it, it was necessary for Melville, because Christianity surrounded him as it surrounds us, to be as Anti-Christ as Ahab was. When he denied Ahab, he lost the Ancient. And Christianity closed in. But he had done his job.

Christ as god contracted his vision. The person of Jesus was another matter. Melville never did come to tolerate the god, and the religion. He merely surrendered to it. The result was creatively a stifling of the myth power in him. The work from *Moby-Dick* on is proof. Melville was the antithesis of Dante. When he permitted himself to try to put his imagination to work in a world of Christian values, as he first did in *Pierre,* it is disaster. *Pierre* is a Christ syllogism: "I hate the world." *The Confidence-Man, Clarel,* and *Billy Budd* are sorites which follow from it.

Melville paid with his flesh too. What he was left with, when he had lost his myth to Christ, was the image of Jesus the person, and he spent forty years trying to turn Him into someone he could love. But those Melville turned to for love, turned away: his mother first, his sister Augusta to her Bible, Hawthorne to his notebook to write: "Herman Melville's linen is none too clean." By the time Melville wrote *Pierre* sex had become to him "the idiot crowned with straw." In the year of his death he published these lines:

> What Cosmic jest or Anarch blunder
> The human integral clove asunder
> And shied the fractions through life's gate? *

After *Moby-Dick* Melville had only Jesus left as the image of what he calls in *Clarel* his "fonder dream of love in man toward man."

* They are from a poem based on an incident of the 1856 trip. It is called "After the Pleasure Party" and is addressed to "Amor Threatening."

There is another curious reflection of woman. It is the only comment Melville made in his copy of *Don Quixote,* which he read, it will be remembered, in 1855-56. It refers to this passage of Cervantes:

> I have already often said it, and now repeat it,
> that a knight-errant without a mistress is like
> a tree without leaves, a building without cement,
> a shadow without a body that causes it.

The note in Melville's hand reads:

> or as Confucius said 'a dog without a master,'
> or, to drop both Cervantes & Confucius parables
> —a god-like mind without a God.

After Ahab his men decline. They are either abstraction, Pierre, or epicene, Billy Budd. Bartleby is an exception—he is parsed into being like the Carpenter in *Moby-Dick*. Benito Cereno is another exception.* The rest are portraits of Jesus: "soft, hermaphroditical Christs." They seek to come together with one another, to close "like halves of apple sweet":

> 'After confidings that should wed
> Our souls in one: —Ah, call me *brother!*'
> So feminine his passionate mood
> Which, long as hungering unfed,
> All else rejected or withstood.

The character of Vine in *Clarel* is a denominator. He has "no trace of passion's soil," is shy and languid, has resisted some "demon" of desire in his "Adam's secret frame"—and shows "disuse of voice." Ahab's Pacific has shrunk to Sodom lake.

The men are also physically flawed, and in mean ways, as if it were Melville's personal revenge on flesh, not the ways of gods and whales who mangled and branded Ahab because he dared to match them in huge contest of elemental force. In *Clarel*, Vine's double, Celio, is a hump-back, a creature of "crook and lump." In *The Confidence-Man* a Negro beggar crawls along the deck of the Mississippi steamboat a cripple, Pip befouled. And the end of them all, Billy or "Baby" Budd, the Latter-day Ishmael, has a stutter. The stutter is the plot. Unable to speak Billy strikes out with his fist and kills his accuser, Claggart, the Master-At-Arms.

It all finally has to do with the throat, SPEECH. Jesus

---

* Both belong, along with the Chola Widow, to that short return, after *Pierre*, to his source of power the Pacific, and the last throw it gave him, from 1853 to 1855. It was the last, to those of us who find the admiration for *Billy Budd* largely a technical one. Men do lose out.

unstrung him. The creator of *Moby-Dick* comes to value the secretive and silent, what lack of love had made his flesh. The American Elizabethan ends by agreeing with a Maurice de Guérin:

> There is more power and beauty in the well-kept secret of one's self and one's thoughts than in the display of a whole heaven that one may have inside one.

Melville's comment, 1869:

> This is the finest verbal statement of a truth which everyone who thinks in these days must have felt.

In *The Confidence-Man,* when Melville used Christ himself directly as a character, he clothed him in white doeskin—and made him a MUTE.

THE EPILOGUE of the '56 *Journal.* Off Cyprus, on his way from the Holyland to Greece, Melville can no more imagine a Venus to have risen from these waters than "on Mt. Olivet that from there Christ rose."

In *Moby-Dick,* in his analysis of what is the hidden nature of the Pacific he had compared its "gentle awful stirrings" to the "fabled undulations of the Ephesian sod over the buried Evangelist St. John." Now, off Patmos, he can "no more realize that St. John had ever had revelations here."

It is the denial. He has faced about, and goes West, to suffer the balk the rest of his days on earth.

A LAST FACT

A LAST FACT

In the back pages of the second of the two notebooks which go to make the *Journal Up the Straits,* among scattered notes which can be identified as directions made by Melville to himself for (1) stories he did not later write but turned into verse, (2) for travel lectures he had to give to help support his family the three years immediately following his return, and (3) for *Clarel,* you will find one note unrelated to the others and untraceable to the *Journal* or later work, a title, a noun (or another title) and a name, as Melville set them down together, in a triangle thus:

Eclipse.

Noah after the Flood.　　　　Cap.[tain] Pollard.
of *Nant.*[ucket]

PART FIVE

Noah

for Constance

The conclusion: Pacific man

There was a story told before Christ of a fisherman of
Boeotia named Glaucus who found an herb to revive fish
as they lay gasping on shore. He ate it himself and was
changed into a sea thing, half fish half man. Melville told
Hawthorne he dated his life from his return from the
Pacific.

MOBY-DICK

CHAPTER CXI

The Pacific

When gliding by the Bashee isles we emerged at last
upon the great South Sea; were it not for other
things, I could have greeted my dear Pacific with un-
counted thanks, for now the long supplication of my

113

youth was answered; that serene ocean rolled east-
ward from me a thousand leagues of blue.

There is, one knows not what sweet mystery about
this sea. . . . .

What the Pacific was to HM:
(1) *an experience of SPACE* most Americans are only
now entering on, 100 years after Melville. Of waters, as
Russia of land, the Pacific gives the sense of immensity.
She is HEART SEA, twin and rival of the HEART-
LAND.

The Pacific is, for an American, the Plains repeated, a
20th century Great West. Melville understood the relation
of the two geographies. A Texas painter settled in Brit-
tany and spent his life on canvases of French fishermen
and the Atlantic Ocean. But the paint, the motion, the
reality turned out to be the Plains. Each canvas was the
Panhandle seen through a screen of sea.

Space has a stubborn way of sticking to Americans,
penetrating all the way in, accompanying them. It is the
exterior fact. The basic exterior act is a BRIDGE. Take
them in order as they came: caravel, prairie schooner,
national road, railway, plane. Now in the Pacific THE
CARRIER. Trajectory. We must go over space, or we
wither.

Exception: the plane. It is a *time* experience, not of
space. *Speed* is its value. The vertical is still will. Flight
does not turn out to be the conquest Daedalus and Da
Vinci imagined it to be. We are (inevitably?), as humans,
Antaean: only in touch with the land and water of the
earth do we keep our WEIGHT, retain POTENTIAL.
Melville kept his by way of the Pacific.

(2) *a comprehension of PAST,* his marriage of spirit to
source. The Pacific turned out to be his Atlantis, the

buried place. The Pacific was "father," older than America, "new-built Californian towns," older than Asia, and Abraham:

> this mysterious, divine Pacific zones the world's whole bulk about; makes all coasts one bay to it; seems the tide-beating heart of earth. Lifted by these eternal swells, you needs must own the seductive god . . .

In Homer the god of genesis was "River Ocean." The Greeks had a myth that Venus was born from the foam of a tidal wave which swept the Aegean after the genitals of Kronos, sickled off by his son, fell into the sea.

Ishmael had to go far down below Ahab's upper earth to find out Ahab's father. Melville's voyage to the Pacific at 21 was a similar quest. The Pacific carried him, much as it did the little Negro Pip, when he drowned, to "won-drous depths where strange shapes of the unwarped primal world glided to and fro before his passive eyes." In *Moby-Dick* Melville speaks of "ocean's utmost bones":

> To have one's hands among the unspeakable foun-dations, ribs, and very pelvis of the world; this is a fearful thing.

In another place, the chapter THE GILDER, he is describing the Pacific, and how land-like a calm of its waters can be, when he bursts out:

> Where is the foundling's father hidden? Our souls are like those orphans whose unwedded mothers die in bearing them; the secret of our paternity lies in their grave, and we must there to learn it.

In the deep, where Pip saw "God's foot on the treadle of the loom," Melville found Ahab's "grim sire," and the

State-secret. Pip came to the surface mad, Melville possessed of his imagination. The Pacific gave him the right of primogeniture.

The Egyptians believed that Osiris, after he was mutilated by his son Seth, had to be buried in the Nile and carried with the mud into the Mediterranean before he could become King of Eternity, Lord of the Underworld, and, his chief attribute, Ruler of the Dead. Noah was Osiris to the Hebrews, and it can be said of him as the Egyptians said: "This is the form of him whom one may not name, Osiris of the mysteries, who springs from the returning waters." In *Mardi* Melville wrote: "Who may call to mind when he was not? To ourselves we all seem coeval with creation. King Noah fathered us all!" After Pacific flood Melville took his dead to be all the fathers and sons of man. The Pacific taught him how to repeat great RITES, of spring. The unceasing ebb and flow took him into a patrimony of Past:

> And meet it is, that over these sea-pastures, wide-rolling watery prairies and Potters' Fields of all four continents, the waves should rise and fall; for here, millions of mixed shades and shadows, drowned dreams, somnambulisms, reveries; all that we call lives and souls, lie dreaming, dreaming still; tossing like slumberers in their beds; the ever-rolling waves but made so by their restlessness.

It was in meadows of brit he found his seed.

The Pacific was also:
(3) *a confirmation of FUTURE*. We think we measure the significance of Columbus and his discoveries. We still fail to calculate the consequence of Magellan's discovery of the Pacific. 3000 years went overboard, and the gains are still unaccomplished.

First, the economic history. Up to the discoveries of the 15th century the Mediterranean remained the center of the world. The basis of commerce was the spices and fine goods of the Orient. It was a trade in luxuries, of high value and small bulk because of limited transportation. The spices varied and made palatable the coarse food of the Middle Ages. The fine goods satisfied a need for comfort, a hunger for beauty, and a desire for display. Venice, then Florence was metropolis.

Columbus operated on the theory: sail to the West and the East will be found. He made the Atlantic the central sea. The mercantilism of 1500-1800 followed. It was the substitution of the Atlantic for the Mediterranean which worked a revolution for England. She was at the center, midway between the Baltic and the Mediterranean and thrust out toward the New World.

With the Pacific opens the NEW HISTORY. Melville: "It rolls the midmost waters of the world, the Indian Ocean and the Atlantic but its arms." The movement into it during the 19th century, of which Melville was a part, makes the third great shift.

Melville felt the movement as American. He understood that America completes her West only on the coast of Asia. He was a sea frontiersman like the whalers Fanning, Delano and other outriders. He was a contemporary in the Pacific of Commodore Charles Wilkes and the U.S. Exploring Expedition, 1838-1842. Later, when Commodore Perry wanted a writer to tell the story of the opening of Japan, Hawthorne recommended Melville as the Pacific man.

I said 3000 years went overboard in the Pacific. I was going back to Homer. The evolution in the use of Ulysses as hero parallels what has happened in economic history.

Homer was an end of the myth world from which the Mediterranean began. But in Ulysses he projected the archetype of the West to follow. It was the creative act of anticipation.

Homer's world was locked tight in River Ocean which circled it, in Anaximander's map, like a serpent with tail in mouth. But in the *Odyssey* Ulysses is already pushing against the limits, seeking a way out. Homer gave his hero the central quality of the men to come: *search, the individual responsible to himself.*

We forget that by 200 B.C. the scope of Western thought had been more or less outlined. The Mediterranean world was already born: the Athenians complain about the vulgar exchanges and busy wharves of Piraeus. Even the range of action has been prospected: Plato has located Atlantis *outside* Homer's terminus, the Pillars of Hercules.

By 1400, in Dante's hands Ulysses is again prospective. He is already an Atlantic man. In the *Inferno* he speaks, a Columbus, to his crew:

> 'O brothers!' I said, 'who through a hundred thousand dangers have reached the West, deny not, to this the brief vigil of your senses that remains, experience of the unpeopled world behind the sun.'

He bends the crew to his purpose, forces them West. They drive through the Pillars, cross the Equator, and after five months on the Atlantic find the New Land only to be destroyed and drowned before they can touch on it.

At the end of the *Paradisio*, when from the seventh sphere the earth is so small its features are obscured as the moon's to us, Dante recognizes one spot on all its surface—that entrance to the West, the Pillars. Dante's last glance is on the threshold to that future Columbus made possible.

The third and final odyssey was Ahab's. The Atlantic crossed, the new land America known, the dream's death lay around the Horn, where West returned to East. The Pacific is the end of the UNKNOWN which Homer's and Dante's Ulysses opened men's eyes to. END of individual responsible only to himself. Ahab is full stop.

Porphyry wrote that the generation of images in the mind is from water.

The three great creations of Melville and *Moby-Dick* are Ahab, The Pacific, and the White Whale.

The son of the father of Ocean was a prophet Proteus, of the changing shape, who, to evade philistine Aristaeus worried about bees, became first a fire, then a flood, and last a wild sea beast.